NEW EDITION

BUSINESS OBJECTIVES

WORKBOOK

Vicki Hollett and Michael Duckworth

Oxford University Press

Oxford University Press,
Great Clarendon Street, Oxford OX2 6DP

Oxford New York
Athens Auckland Bangkok Bogotá Buenos Aires Cape Town
Chennai Dar es Salaam Delhi Florence Hong Kong Istanbul
Karachi Kolkata Kuala Lumpur Madrid Melbourne Mexico City
Mumbai Nairobi Paris São Paulo Shanghai Singapore Taipei
Tokyo Toronto Warsaw

with associated companies in
Berlin Ibadan

OXFORD and OXFORD ENGLISH are trade marks of
Oxford University Press

ISBN 0 19 451392 0

© Oxford University Press 1996

First published 1996
Tenth impression 2001

Printed in Hong Kong

The publishers would like to thank the following for their
permission to reproduce photographs:

James Davis Travel Photography: p 14
Hewlett Packard Ltd: p 20
IBM (UK) Ltd: p 22
Mazda Cars (UK) Ltd: p 20
Rex Features: p 21
Sparham / Network: p 52

Illustrations by:

Jackie Harland
Nigel Paige
Technical Graphics Dept (OUP)

We would also like to thank the following for their permission
to reproduce copyright material:

Would you like to hear some music while you hold?
by C. Barsotti, © 1979 The New Yorker Magazine, Inc: p 8
*Well, if I called the wrong number, why did you answer the
phone?* James Thurber Literary Properties: p 12

Design: B G Prentiss, The Art Room, The Old School

Acknowledgements

The authors and publisher would like to thank the following
for permission to use articles, extracts, or adaptations of
copyright material:

p 28: Nicholas Brealey Publishing. Extract from *Mind Your
Manners, Managing Business Cultures in Europe*, by John Mole
(Nicholas Brealey Publishing, London 1995)

p 4: British MENSA: advertisement

p 20: Ewan MacNaughton Associates on behalf of The
Telegraph plc: extract from 'Fold up car that fits in a suitcase'
by Robert Whymant. The *Daily Telegraph*, 9 May 1991, © The
Telegraph plc, London, 1991

p 14: Monaco Government Tourist and Convention Office:
brochure extract

p 61: Penguin Books Ltd and the author c/o Rogers, Coleridge
& White, 20 Powis Mews, London W11 1JN: adapted extract
from *The Book of Heroic Failures* by Stephen Pile (Penguin
Books, 1990) copyright © Stephen Pile, 1979, 1989.

p 38: Sony Europe Finance plc: company information

Despite every effort to trace and contact copyright holders
prior to publication this has not been possible in some cases.
If notified, the publisher will be pleased to rectify any errors or
omissions at the earliest opportunity.

Contents

1 Meeting People

1 First meetings

Put this conversation into the correct order.

- [ ] **Elaine** Please call me Elaine.
- [ ] **Paul** Morning, Jenny. How are you?
- [ ] **Jenny** Yes, it is. Let me introduce you … Excuse me, Mrs Redford. May I introduce you to Paul Carroll?
- [1] **Jenny** Good morning, Paul.
- [ ] **Paul** Pleased to meet you, Mrs Redford.
- [ ] **Jenny** Fine, thanks, and you?
- [ ] **Paul** And please call me Paul.
- [ ] **Elaine** How do you do?
- [ ] **Paul** Fine. Is that Mrs Redford over there?

2 Jobs

Complete the sentences using the following phrases.

for Lego	in computers	a doctor	an accountant
for Canon	an estate agent	in construction	a solicitor

1 I'm _____ . I buy and sell houses.

2 I'm _____ . I work for IBM.

3 I'm _____ . I specialize in corporate law.

4 I work _____ . We produce photocopiers, fax machines, and other

office equipment.

5 I'm _____ . I work at Guy's Hospital in London.

6 I work _____ , the Danish toy manufacturer.

7 I'm _____ . I work in the financial services section.

8 I'm _____ . I work on building projects in the Middle East.

3 Job titles

A Think of three people you work with. Write their names and job titles.

	Name	**Job title**
Example	*Nadine Calvo*	*Human Resources Director*
1	_____	_____
2	_____	_____
3	_____	_____

B Describe briefly what one of the people does at work.

Example *Mme Calvo is our Human Resources Director. She is responsible for all personnel matters. She recruits new staff, liaises with health and safety representatives, organizes training courses, and also deals with retirement arrangements.*

_____

_____

_____

C Now describe your job. Say what you do at work.

_____

_____

_____

4 Companies

Match these companies to their main business activities, the countries in which they are based, and the countries' currencies. Use the information below.

> South Korea   Japan   Finland   ~~Italy~~   Switzerland   France   USA   Denmark
> rubber products   forestry products   shipbuilding   food
> photographic equipment   electronics   beverages   computers
> kröne   franc   ~~lira~~   dollar   yen   markka   won   Swiss franc

Company	Main business activity	Country	Currency
Olivetti	computers	Italy	lira
Mitsui			
Jacobs Suchard			
Eastman Kodak			
Daewoo	electronics		
Michelin			
Rauma-Repola			
Carlsberg			

5 Asking questions

A Read this conversation between two lawyers at a conference. Fill in the blanks with these question words:

> who   what   how   why   when   where

Klaus   _____ ¹ do you do? I'm Klaus Binder.

Peter   Nice to meet you. Peter Green.

Klaus   Ah! You're giving a talk on satellite launches.

Peter   That's right. _____ ² are you from, Mr Binder?

Klaus   Berlin.

Peter   And _____ ³ do you work for?

Klaus   Sky Television.

Peter   Ah, yes! You're giving a talk on transmission systems.

Klaus   That's right.

Peter   I'd like to hear it. _____ ⁴ is it?

Klaus   After lunch. _____ ⁵ don't you come along?

Peter   I'd like to. _____ ⁶ time does it start?

B Ask Peter some questions about Klaus. Complete the conversation.

You	Who is that man over there?
Peter	His name is Klaus Binder.
You	_____ [1]?
Peter	Berlin.
You	_____ [2]?
Peter	No, he's Austrian, actually, but he was born in Germany.
You	_____ [3]?
Peter	Sky Television.
You	_____ [4]?
Peter	He's an engineer.
You	_____ [5]?
Peter	He's the Technical Director.

6 Boardroom puzzle

Three business people are at a meeting. From the information below, work out everyone's name, nationality, job, and where they are sitting.

- The Managing Director is at the head of the table.
- The people come from three different countries.
- They have three different jobs. There's the MD, an accountant, and a lawyer.
- The Accountant comes from Switzerland.
- The Englishman is on the MD's right-hand side.
- Peter comes from Germany.
- The Lawyer's name is Nathan.
- Bernadette is opposite the man from England.

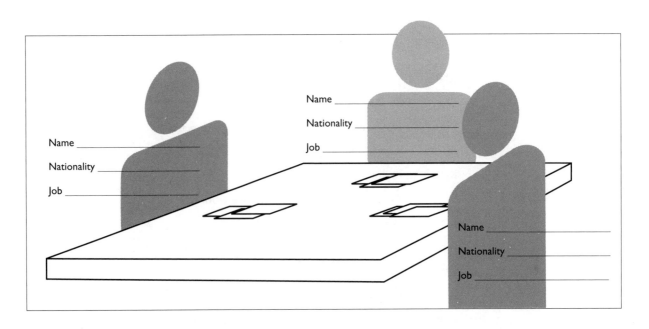

Name _____
Nationality _____
Job _____

Name _____
Nationality _____
Job _____

Name _____
Nationality _____
Job _____

7 Commuting

A Read this passage about a commuter. Think about what information is missing.

Annie Clayden lives in Norwich but she works in _____ ¹, a hundred miles away. She leaves home at _____ ² in the morning and she travels to work by _____ ³. It takes _____ ⁴ but she enjoys the journey. She travels with _____ ⁵ and she doesn't get bored because _____ ⁶.

B What questions can you ask to get the missing information?

1 Where _____ ?
2 What time _____ ?
3 How _____ ?
4 How long _____ ?
5 Who _____ ?
6 Why _____ ?

C Here is the missing information. Now use it to complete the passage.

two and a half hours	London	three friends
they all play *Trivial Pursuit*	6.30	train

8 Replies

Match these questions to the correct reply.

1 Where do you come from?   a About half an hour.
2 How do you do?   b Spain.
3 How are you?   c I'm Swiss.
4 How long does it take?   d Cathay Pacific.
5 Who do you work for?   e No, I'm from Canada.
6 What line of business are you in? f I'm an accountant.
7 What nationality are you?   g Advertising.
8 How do you get to work?   h How do you do?
9 Are you American?   i By train.
10 What do you do?   j Fine thanks and you?

9 Reading

A Match the sentences below to make rules like the one in the example.

Example   *Managers don't make mistakes. They test their staff.*

1 Managers don't arrive late.   a They collect information.
2 Managers don't read   b They think with their eyes shut.
  the newspaper.   c They invest in new technology.
3 Managers don't forget things.   d They are unavoidably delayed.
4 Managers don't sleep.   e If they do, they're the managers' ideas.
5 Managers don't buy new toys.   f Their employees forget to remind
6 Employees don't have good ideas.   them.

B Can you make any more rules?

2 Telephoning

I Pronunciation

A Match the letters that have the same vowel sound.

1	B	a	U
2	I	b	P
3	D	c	Y
4	Q	d	K
5	M	e	G
6	J	f	S

B Match the letters with a word that has the same vowel sound.

1	O	a	free
2	R	b	pay
3	U	c	car
4	V	d	toe
5	I	e	shoe
6	J	f	fly

C Now look at the abbreviations below. They are grouped by sound. Find the abbreviation which sounds different from the other three.

Example   CBI   BDI   PTY   (PTE)   (The last sound is different)

1	GDP	PST	GMT	GNP
2	MIT	NEC	NYC	FIT
3	VAT	CAP	BKG	PLC
4	EGM	CIF	DCF	PPS
5	COD	BOT	FOB	POD

2 Making calls

Match these comments to their replies.

1 Sorry, could you spell that?
2 Could I speak to Mrs Fenton, please?
3 Could you take a message?
4 I'm afraid the line's busy at the moment.
5 I'm sorry but he's away this week.
6 Could you repeat that?

a Yes, it's 0181 432 9191.
b That's OK. I'll hold.
c I'll call back next week, then.
d Speaking.
e Yes of course. I'll get a pen.
f Yes, it's M-E-E-U-W-S.

Would you like to hear some music while you hold?

3 On the line

Choose the correct words in italics to complete the telephone conversation.

A Fenton Engineering.
B *Number / Extension* [1] 473, please.
A I'm afraid the line's *broken / engaged* [2]. Will you hold?
B Yes.

A The line's free now. I'll *put / connect* [3] you through.
B Thank you.
C Paint shop.
B I'd like to speak to Mrs Isaacs.
C *Who's / Whose* [4] calling, please?
B Jacques Duval.
C *Wait / Hold on* [5], M Duval. I'll *bring / get* [6] her.

C I'm *afraid / regret* [7] she's in a meeting. Do you want to call *up / back* [8] later?
B No, it's urgent. Could you *leave / take* [9] a message?
C Yes, *I will / of course* [10].
B *May / Could* [11] you ask her to call me back?
C Does she have your number?
B No. It's Paris – the *code / area* [12] is 00 331 then the number is 46 58 93 94. Could you *say / read* [13] that back to me?
C 00 331 46 58 93 94.
B That's right.
C *Anything / What* [14] else?
B No, that's *anything / all* [15]. Thank you very much.
C You're *welcome / fine* [16].
B Goodbye.

4 Requests

A Put these phrases into two groups:

| Could you ...? | Can I ...? | Would you ...? |
| May I ...? | Can you ...? | Could I ...? |

asking other people to do things	asking if it's OK to do things

B Use the phrases from Part A in sentences below.

Example What would you say to a customer if you wanted to use their phone?
May I use your phone?

What would you say:

1 to ask a friend to tell you the time?

2 to a colleague if you wanted to smoke in their office?

3 if you wanted a friend to give you a lift to the station?

4 if you wanted to borrow your boss's copy of the production plan?

_____

5 if you wanted to copy a file from a colleague's computer?

_____

6 if you wanted a colleague to lend you a book?

_____

5 Wordcheck

Complete the puzzle and find the keyword in 14 down.

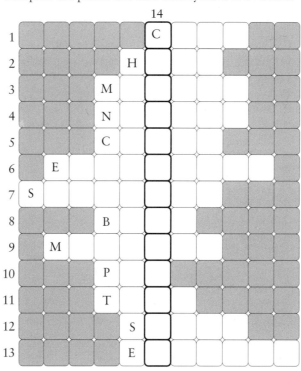

Across

1 I'll _____ back later. (4)

2 The line's busy. Will you _____ ? (4)

3 Could you hold on a _____ and I'll get a pen. (6)

4 My new _____ will be 0171 335 2378. (6)

5 _____ I leave a message? (5)

6 May I have _____ 3285, please? (9)

7 Good afternoon. Paul Moran _____ . (8)

8 I'll ask Mr Travers to call you _____ as soon as possible. (4)

9 Would you like me to take a _____ ? (7)

10 Could you _____ me through to Miss Nixon, please? (3)

11 Good morning, _____ is Richard Bowers. (4)

12 I'm _____ , but Mr Laws is away all week. (5)

13 The line is _____ . Can I ask her to call you back? (7)

Down

14 One of the keys to successful management. (13)

6 Writing letters

A Complete the following letter using the correct word or phrase from the list below.

> I would be grateful …
>
> Thank you for your help.
>
> I look forward to hearing from …
>
> I am writing to confirm …
>
> Could you possibly … ?
>
> Yours …
>
> With reference to …

Dear Mr Hendrickson,

_____ [1] our telephone conversation today,

_____ [2] that I will be in Sweden from 11 - 14 June.

_____ [3] if you could arrange for me to visit the Technical Department in Stockholm. If possible, I would also like to meet Mr Elmqvist.

_____ [4] also send me a list of any hotels near Head Office that you would recommend, and I will make the bookings from here?

_____ [5]

_____ [6] you.

_____ [7] sincerely,

M K Vernon

M K Vernon

B Now complete the reply using a word or phrase from the list below:

Dear Mr Vernon,

_____ [1] May 21.

_____ [2] give you details of the arrangements for your visit.

_____ [3] show you round the Technical Department when you arrive. I have arranged a visit for Monday June 12 at 11.00 am.

_____ [4] Mr Elmqvist will not be here when you come, but his deputy, Mr Karlsbad, will be pleased to meet you.

_____ [5] a list of hotels near Head Office. I would particularly recommend the Sheraton, which most of our visitors enjoy.

_____ [6] we can help in any way.

_____ [7] in June.

Yours _____ [8],

K K Hendrickson

K K Hendrickson

> I am afraid that …
>
> Please contact us again if …
>
> Thank you for your letter of …
>
> I am enclosing …
>
> I would be delighted to …
>
> … sincerely
>
> I look forward to meeting you …
>
> I am writing to …

7 Reading

Read these extracts from telephone calls. Who do you think is talking? What do you think they are talking about?

1   **A**   I'll see you outside the bank at 11.30 then.
    B   No, I said 11.28.
    A   OK, 11.28.
    B   And don't forget to change the number-plates.

2   **A**   It's Mr Carter on line 4.
    B   Not again! Could you tell him I'm busy, Mary.
    A   I did, but he says he'll wait.
    B   Oh, all right then. Put him through.

3   **A**   I'm afraid no one is available to take your call.
    B   Oh no, I hate these things.
    A   Please leave your name and number after the tone.
    B   Er hello … er … I'll call back later.

4   **A**   Darling, it's me. Can you talk?
    B   Wait a minute. Yes, I think so, but be quick.
    A   I can't stop thinking about you.
    B   Thank you for calling, Mr Jackson. I'll put a catalogue in the post for you right away.

5   **A**   I'm on my last unit.
    B   Hold on, Jane, I'll get a pencil … OK.
    A   I'm on 0181 …
    B   Oh no!

6   **A**   All in all the legal fees come to £30,000.
    B   That's very reasonable. That's one three, I hope.
    A   No, Mr Brown, three zero, I'm afraid.
    B   What? For three weeks' work? You must be joking!

Well, if I called the wrong number, why did you answer the phone?

3 Companies

1 Current projects

A Match the two halves of these sentences.

1 The British Airports Authority are building ...

   a a joint venture agreement.

2 NCC are strengthening their position in Europe by making ...

   b from Grosvenor House to the Barbican Centre.

3 BAT Industries and Pecs are negotiating ...

   c new financial products.

4 Due to the shortage of space, the Lonrho Group are moving their AGM ...

   d a new passenger terminal at London Heathrow.

5 SKF are establishing manufacturing operations ...

   e a number of strategic acquisitions.

6 Crédit Agricole, a leading French banking group, are diversifying to provide ...

   f in Eastern Europe.

B Now write two sentences about your company's current activities:

_____

_____

2 Present Continuous

A journalist from the *New York Times* is phoning a friend in London. Complete the dialogue, using the verbs in italics. Use the Present Continuous tense.

do   write   stay (x2)   call   visit   collect

Peter   Peter Warner speaking.

Hilary   Peter. Hello, this is Hilary.

Peter   Hilary, how nice to hear from you! Where _____ you

_____ [1] from?

Hilary   London. I _____ _____ [2] at the Hilton.

Peter   Really? What _____ you _____ [3] in London?

Hilary   I _____ _____ [4] some information for an article that

I _____ _____ [5] about the London Stock Exchange.

Peter   That's wonderful. Is David with you?

Hilary   Yes, he _____ _____ [6] his London office at the same

time.

Peter   How long _____ you both _____ [7] ?

Hilary   Just a week.

Peter   I hope you've got time to come and see us.

BUSINESS OBJECTIVES

3 Facilities

The Monte Carlo Convention Centre and Auditorium at the foot of the Casino terraces overlooks the port of Monaco.

Meeting Rooms
- Congress Hall: seating for 1,100
- Exhibition space: 1,800m²; 100 stands
- 4 Meeting rooms: seating for 70 - 180

Services
- Simultaneous translation in 9 languages
- Press Rcom
- Telephone, Fax, and Telex facilities
- Secretarial offices
- Organizer's office
- Lobby bar for coffee breaks or receptions
- Winter Garden "Troparium"
- Close to 2 car parks

Hotels
Within walking distance of the centre are 6 hotels of the highest international standard with all major facilities.

How to get to the centre

By train: All international trains stop at Monaco Station.

By road: From Germany and Switzerland there are non-stop motorways. From Britain and France use the Autoroute du Soleil.

By air: The International Airport of Nice–Côte d'Azur is 22 km from Monaco. There is a regular helicopter service which takes 7 minutes. All the main cities of Western Europe are less than 2 hours away.

Amsterdam	1 hour 40 minutes
London	1 hour 50 minutes
Brussels	1 hour 40 minutes
Madrid	1 hour 45 minutes
Frankfurt	1 hour 25 minutes
Paris	1 hour 15 minutes
Geneva	55 minutes
Rome	1 hour

A Complete these questions using *Is there … ?* or *Are there … ?*

1 _____ a translation service?

2 _____ a press room?

3 _____ telephone, fax, and telex facilities?

4 _____ secretarial services?

5 _____ anywhere to go during coffee breaks?

6 How many meeting rooms _____ _____?

7 _____ _____ plenty of parking space?

B Now match the above questions to these replies.

a Yes, there are secretarial offices in the complex.
b There are five. The largest holds 1,100 people.
c Yes, there's a lobby bar.
d Yes, there are two car parks nearby.
e Yes, there's a special room for journalists.
f Yes. There are good telecommunication facilities.
g Yes, there is, in 9 languages.

14 UNIT 3

4 Asking questions

Ask and answer more questions about the Monte Carlo Convention Centre. Put the words in the right order to make the questions.

Example   Centre   Convention   is   the   Where?
Q *Where is the Convention Centre?*
A *It's in Monaco.*

1 are   Centre   hotels   How   many   near   the   there?

Q _____

A _____

2 airport   an   Centre   Is   near   the   there?

Q _____

A _____

3 airport   far   from   How   is   Monaco   Nice?

Q _____

A _____

4 by   does   get   helicopter   How   it   long   take   there   to?

Q _____

A _____

5 does   fly   from   How   it   long   Madrid   take   there   to ?

Q _____

A _____

6 links   there   road   Are   and   good   rail?

Q _____

A _____

5 Present Simple and Continuous

Read these two paragraphs about Hilary Morey:

> Hilary Morey is a journalist. She lives in New York and works for the *New York Times*. She writes for the financial section of the paper.
>
> At the moment she's visiting London, doing some research for an article she's writing. She's staying at the Hilton with her husband, David.

Write two similar paragraphs about yourself.
Note: We use the Present Simple tense to describe permanent or long-term situations, but we use the Present Continuous tense to describe temporary or current activities.

_____

_____

_____

_____

_____

_____

6 Saying numbers How do you pronounce the numbers in these sentences? Write them in words.

Example We have 13 factories. _thirteen_ _____

1 I joined the company in 1990. _____

2 The meeting begins at 10.45. _____

3 The next Sales Conference starts on 21 January. _____

4 Value Added Tax is now 17 $\frac{1}{2}$%. _____

5 The price is £34.50. _____

6 A pint is 0.5683 litres. _____

7 Reading Read these profiles of well-known companies. Rearrange the letters to make the company name.

1 This company's headquarters are in Michigan, but it earns a lot of its annual $6,562 million revenue outside the USA. It sells its products in 130 countries and has about half of the European breakfast cereal market. Its leading brand names are Cornflakes, Rice Krispies, and Frosties.

LELGSKOG _____

2 This company manufactures mice! Computer mice. They also develop disk-operating and application software. Their annual sales are $4,649 million and they have 15,257 employees. It is famous for its 'Windows' operating system.

RTOOIMCSF _____

3 This is one of the world's top chemical companies. It has sales outlets in 170 countries and production facilities in thirty-nine. It spends nearly DM2,000 per year on research and development and produces more than 8,000 products. The best known of these are audio and video cassettes.

FSBA _____

4 This company operates in 3 major areas: beverages, snack foods, and restaurants. With a turnover of over $28 billion, it is the world's largest producer of crisps and has the largest number of franchised restaurants in the world. Everyone knows their Pizza Hut and Kentucky Fried Chicken restaurants. Their brands include Fritos corn chips, Ruffles potato chips, and Walkers crisps. Their most famous product is a fizzy drink.

SEPOCIP _____

5 This company is the largest tyre-maker in the world and has a 20% share of the world market. Based in France, it has 69 plants and rubber plantations in Brazil, the Ivory Coast and Nigeria. 96% of its sales come from tyres and wheels and only 4% from other products such as guidebooks.

CELMIHNI _____

8 Wordcheck

Find the hidden words in this square. You can read from left to right, from top to bottom and diagonally. Use the clues below to help you.

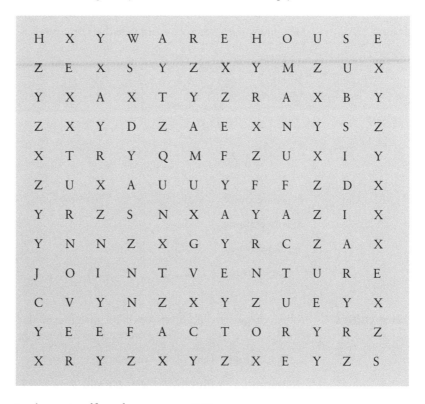

H	X	Y	W	A	R	E	H	O	U	S	E
Z	E	X	S	Y	Z	X	Y	M	Z	U	X
Y	X	A	X	T	Y	Z	R	A	X	B	Y
Z	X	Y	D	Z	A	E	X	N	Y	S	Z
X	T	R	Y	Q	M	F	Z	U	X	I	Y
Z	U	X	A	U	U	Y	F	F	Z	D	X
Y	R	Z	S	N	X	A	Y	A	Z	I	X
Y	N	N	Z	X	G	Y	R	C	Z	A	X
J	O	I	N	T	V	E	N	T	U	R	E
C	V	Y	N	Z	X	Y	Z	U	E	Y	X
Y	E	E	F	A	C	T	O	R	Y	R	Z
X	R	Y	Z	X	Y	Z	X	E	Y	Z	S

1 the main office of a company (12)
2 the people who work for a company – its employees (5)
3 a large building where goods are stored (9)
4 a building where goods are made (7)
5 a person who buys and uses goods or services (8)
6 a company that is controlled by another company (10)
7 to produce in large quantities with machinery (11)
8 the total sales of a company (8)
9 a group of products sold by one company (5)
10 a regular payment for use of land, building, offices, machinery, etc. (4)
11 a co-operative operation between two companies (5, 7)

We are always looking for new markets for our products.

4 Exchanging Information

1 Opposites

Here are some adjectives. Complete their opposites as in number 1.

1 good   bad

2 big   s _ _ _ _

3 q _ _ _ _   noisy

4 fast   s _ _ _

5 n _ _   old

6 y _ _ _ _   old

7 interesting   b _ _ _ _ _ _

8 entertaining d _ _ _

9 expensive   c _ _ _ _

10 expensive   g _ _ _ v _ _ _ _

2 Describing things

Match the groups of adjectives, 1–10, with one of the nouns on the right that they can describe. Then add one more word to each group, as in the example.

1 fascinating	long	interesting	*informative*	a car
2 fast	portable	user-friendly	_____	a company
3 wonderful	hot	humid	_____	secretary
4 attractive	high	competitive	_____	a computer
5 friendly	luxurious	five-star	_____	an office
6 reliable	punctual	bilingual	_____	a presentation
7 noisy	smoky	open-plan	_____	weather
8 efficient	small	multinational	_____	a hotel
9 economical	fast	comfortable	_____	a letter
10 urgent	brief	short	_____	a price

3 More adjectives

A sales representative is talking to her boss. Choose the correct adjective in each sentence.

1 Thank you very much for a very *interested / interesting* presentation.

2 We were all very *interesting / interested*.

3 Of course, we're *exciting / excited* to hear about this new product.

4 But the figures are a little *confusing / confused*.

5 We were *surprising / surprised* by next year's sales targets. They're very high.

6 And this present recession is very *worrying / worried*.

7 Anyway, it was a *fascinating / fascinated* presentation.

8 And we were all *amusing / amused* by your joke at the end.

4 Measurements

Complete the sentences with the right dimensions from the list below.

1,615 m deep	8.85 km high	2,889 pages thick
300.5 m tall	3,460 km long	70–72 beats per minute

1   The Eiffel Tower is _____

2   The Grand Canyon is _____ .

3   Mount Everest is _____ .

4   The Great Wall of China is _____ .

5   The normal adult pulse rate is _____ .

6   The Houston, Texas telephone directory was _____ .

5 Wordcheck

A Look at the lists and circle the word that is different from the others.

Example   wood   (chair)   plastic   steel

1   crate   paper   box   carton

2   a mistake   a phone call   a suggestion   a job

3   comfortable   friendly   efficient   happy

4   height   length   depth   wide

B Now choose the correct words you circled for these sentences:

Example   *Chair is different because it's furniture. The others are materials to make furniture.*

1   _____ is different because it's packaging material, not a container.

2   _____ is different because the opposite starts with *in-*, not *un-*.

3   _____ is different because it's an adjective, not a noun.

4   _____ is different because we do it, we don't make it.

6 Car problems

Complete this story. Put *was, were, wasn't* and *weren't* in the correct spaces.

A friend of mine was a car mechanic in a garage and one of his customers _____[1] a lovely grey-haired old lady. All the mechanics _____[2] very fond of her because she gave good tips, but they _____[3] fond of her car. Most Morris Minors are reliable but hers _____[4] a real problem. It _____[5] impossible to start in summer, it jumped along the road like a kangaroo and it _____[6] very thirsty. All the mechanics _____[7] puzzled by it. They checked the fuel pipes but they _____[8] the problem. They checked the engine but it _____[9] that. The car _____[10] in and out of the garage every week but they _____[11] never able to locate the problem. One day my friend asked the lady to take him for a drive in the car so he could listen for any strange noises. She _____[12] happy to help and jumped in to the driver's seat and put on her seat belt. Then she pulled out the choke and hung her handbag on it. The mystery _____[13] solved. That _____[14] why the car _____[15] so thirsty.

7 Product specifications

Memory 1MB built-in RAM	**Weight** 5.3kg
Dimensions *Width:* 447mm *Height:* 218mm *Depth:* 394mm	

Look at the product specifications. Write questions to go with the answers below.

Example   Q   How big is the memory?
           A   It's 1 MB.

1   Q _____

    A   It's 394 mm.

2   Q _____

    A   It's 447 mm.

3   Q _____

    A   It's 218 mm.

4   Q _____

    A   It weighs 5.3 kg.

5   Q _____

    A   About £350.

8 Reading

Would you like to buy this product? Read the article and find out.

THIS WEEK

Fold-up car that fits in a suitcase

Engineers at Mazda, the Japanese car company, have designed a car you can fold in half and carry around in a suitcase.

The 'Suitcase Car' is only 81cm x 61cm x 25cm when folded, but opens to a length of 117cm, a width of 102 cm, and a height of 41cm. The vehicle weighs 30kg and costs £900 to build. It only takes one minute to set up for the road.

The car is propelled by a specially-designed, two cycle single-cylinder engine and it has a maximum speed of just under 30km an hour.

The invention won first prize in a contest arranged by Mazda to encourage original ideas from its employees. The winning team of seven engineers said they had always wanted to build a car that could be folded up in a traffic jam and carried away. The engineers also wanted to design a car that people could take on aeroplanes.

The portable car was not made for driving on roads, so it is only the first step towards achieving the engineers' goal. A Mazda spokesman said the company had no plans to mass produce the 'Suitcase Car'. ∎

5 Reporting

1 A career history

Margaret Thatcher

1925 Born in Grantham, Lincolnshire, Margaret Hilda, daughter of Alfred Roberts, a grocer. Later attended Grantham Girls' School. Studied Chemistry at Somerville College, Oxford.

1947–51 Worked as a research chemist.

1951 Married Denis Thatcher, a London-based business executive.

1951–54 Studied law. Specialized in tax law.

1953 Had twins, a son and daughter, Mark and Carol.

1954 Qualified as a lawyer.

1959 Elected Member of Parliament for Finchley.

1970–74 Member of Cabinet – Secretary of State for Education and Science.

1975 Elected leader of the Conservative Party. First woman to lead a British political party.

1979 Conservatives defeated Labour Party in General Election. Became Prime Minister (first woman, 52nd Prime Minister).

1982 Retained control of the Falkland Islands by use of military force.

1983 Won a General Election.

1984 Survived IRA bomb attack at the Grand Hotel, Brighton. Visited the USA.

1987 Won a third General Election.

1990 Replaced as Prime Minister by John Major.

1992 Became a life peer.

1993 Published a book, *The Downing Street Years 1979-1990.*

A English verbs ending in *-ed* are pronounced in three different ways:

/d/ *died, lived*
/t/ *produced, established*
/ɪd/ *started, expanded*

B Group these words from the career history according to their pronunciation.

attended	studied	worked	married	specialized	elected
defeated	retained	survived	visited	published	replaced

/d/ _____ _____ _____ _____ _____

/t/ _____ _____ _____

/ɪd/ _____ _____ _____ _____

2 Describing a career   Complete the text using the Past Simple tense of the verbs in brackets.

The founder of IBM

■ Thomas J. Watson Senior _____[1](begin) his business career as a sewing machine salesman and later, when he _____[2](become) President of IBM, he _____[3](use) his sales techniques to promote the company's name. There _____[4](be) IBM anthems, IBM songbooks, IBM regulation clothes, and the company motto, 'Think' _____[5](appear) on every wall in the organization.

■ When Watson _____[6](join) IBM in 1914, the company _____[7](be) almost broke. Under his leadership, it _____[8](grow) beyond all expectations, and _____[9](adopt) a leading position in the information-processing industry. So how did he do it?

■ Watson _____[10](believe) that the way to win a man's loyalty is to build up his self-respect. So under his management, IBM employees _____[11](earn) above-average salaries and good pensions. In return, he _____[12](demand) loyalty and enthusiasm. Everyone _____[13](work) long hours.

■ Until the 1950s, IBM never _____[14](sell) machines. They just _____[15](rent) them to customers. Watson _____[16](insist) on this policy, and it _____[17](help) the company to survive the Depression of the 1930s. He _____[18](have) a strong personality and _____[19](make) all the major decisions himself. As many as forty top people _____[20](report) to him personally. Watson _____[21](think) that a manager should be an assistant to his men, and IBM _____[22](run) no management training schools in his day. The only advice he _____[23](give) was: 'You're promoted to Assistant Manager. Be careful with people, don't swear, and wear a white shirt.'

3 Irregular verbs

Study the words in column C. What verbs can you use with them? Write the infinitive and past forms of the verb in columns A and B. Some letters are given to help you.

	A infinitive	B past simple	C
1	break	broke	… a contract, … a promise, … a glass
2	s _ _ _	_ _ _ t	… an invoice, … a letter, … a fax
3	_ _ y	_ _ _ d	… in cash, … a bill, … a dividend
4	_ _ k _	_ _ _ e	… a profit, … a mistake, … an appointment
5	_ _ a _	_ e _ _	… a report, … a book, … the newspaper
6	_ l _	_ _ e _	… business class, … by helicopter, … by Concorde
7	f _ _ _	_ _ l _	… sick, … tired, … happy
8	_ _ _ r _	_ _ _ _ _ t	… a lesson, … a language, … something new

4 Dates and times

Write down when you last did these things. Use *on*, *in* or *at* in your answers.

1 When did you last go on holiday?   *In the summer.* _____

2 When did you get to work this morning? _____

3 When did you last go to the dentist? _____

4 When was your last birthday? _____

5 When did you last go abroad? _____

6 When did you last go to a meeting? _____

7 When did you last get paid? _____

8 When did you start this exercise? _____

5 Questions

A Here are some questions and answers about a business trip. Complete the questions using words from the list below. Then match each question to the correct reply.

Who   Was   Where   When   Did   How   Which   What   ~~Why~~

1 _____ did you go?   a Some of our agents.

2 *Why* did you go?   b Yes, it was very useful.

3 _____ did you meet?   c Yes, a few.

4 _____ you make any useful contacts?   d To do some market research.

5 _____ long did you stay?   e The Sheraton.

6 _____ did you get back?   f Gulf Air.

7 _____ airline did you fly with?   g Dubai.

8 _____ hotel did you stay in?   h A week.

9 _____ the trip a success?   i On Thursday.

B Here are some answers but what are the questions? Make questions using the verbs in italics.

Example Who *did you write to?* I *wrote* to Mr. Jackson.

1 When _____?

I *phoned* her yesterday afternoon.

2 Why _____?

He *left* because he was offered a better job.

3 Where _____?

He *went* to London.

4 How _____?

It *cost* over £300.

5 Did _____?

No, I didn't *see* the report.

6 How _____?

I *stayed* at the exhibition for two hours.

7 Who _____?

I *spoke* to the General Manager's secretary.

8 What _____?

The weather *was* great.

6 Your career

Write a short paragraph about your past business experience and career.
Give details about:

where you went to school
what you did after you left school
when you started your first job
what you did, what your responsibilities were
what happened to you between your first job and your present one

6 Socializing

1 Welcoming a visitor Complete the conversation using the phrases below.

try some Greek food	eat anything on the plane
the restaurant or the hotel first	sort of food do you like
have a good flight to meet you	your first visit

A Mr Hathaway?

B Yes, that's right. You must be Mr Striebel.

A Yes. Pleased _____ [1].

B And you.

A Is this _____ [2] to Athens?

B Yes, I've always wanted to come but I never had the chance.

A Good, I can show you around. Did you _____ [3]?

B Yes, it was fine, thanks. No delays or problems.

A Good. Let me take your case. The car's just outside. Did you

_____ [4]?

B No, I wasn't hungry.

A Well, what would you like to do? Shall we go to _____ [5]?

B The hotel, I think. I'd like a shower. We can eat later, if that's OK.

A That's fine by me. What _____ [6]? We've got a good choice

of restaurants here – French, Italian, and Greek, of course.

B I'd like to _____ [7].

A Good, that's settled. I'll drop you off now and come and pick you up again at

about eight.

2 Socializing Match the comments with a suitable reply.

1	Another drink?	a	Germany.
2	Where do you come from?	b	Not too bad, thanks.
3	Thank you very much indeed.	c	Yes, we met last week.
4	Hello, Steve! How are things?	d	Just a few words.
5	How many sugars?	e	No, thanks, I'm driving.
6	Can you speak French?	f	Sorry, I don't smoke.
7	Do you know Mr Davis?	g	Just one, please.
8	You haven't got a light, have you?	h	You're welcome.

3 Wordcheck   Look at the lists and circle the word that is different from the others. Then explain why.

The other three are

Example   prawn   lobster   crab   (veal)   *types of shellfish* _____

1 roast   fry   steak   grill   _____

2 mashed   frozen   french-fried   baked   _____

3 peach   potato   melon   raspberry   _____

4 pea   salmon   sole   plaice   _____

5 lamb   pork   bacon   ham   _____

6 cream   margarine   butter   milk   _____

7 cauliflower   sprouts   carrots   bread   _____

8 medium   rare   well-done   cooked   _____

4 Menus   **A** Match the nouns below with the correct pictures. Then decide whether the nouns are countable (C) or uncountable (U).

1 bread   _U_

2 wine   ____

3 tomato   ____

4 biscuit   _C_

5 butter   ____

6 cheese   ____

7 apple   ____

8 sugar   ____

9 water   ____

10 soup   ____

11 grape   ____

Check some of your answers in a dictionary. A good dictionary will tell you if a noun is countable or uncountable, or look at p. 174 in the Student's Book for further information.

B In your own language, write down the names of five dishes which are popular in your country. Then describe these dishes for an English person you are taking to lunch.

Example   Escargots à l'ail *are snails cooked in butter and garlic.*

1 _____

2 _____

3 _____

4 _____

5 _____

5 Free time

A Complete these questions with *do*, *play* or *go*, then answer them.

Example   Do you go jogging?   *No, I don't.* _____

1 Do you _____ tennis?   _____

2 Do you _____ sailing?   _____

3 Do you _____ swimming?   _____

4 Do you _____ football?   _____

5 Do you _____ yoga?   _____

B Write true sentences about your free-time activities, using the words in italics and the ideas below.

| always | usually | often | sometimes | not often | never |

Example   *I don't often watch television.*

1 television _____

2 take work home _____

3 cinema _____

4 tennis/squash _____

5 read _____

6 go to bars _____

7 golf _____

8 restaurants _____

6 Social expressions

Match these comments to when you would say them.

1 Many happy returns of the day.   a When meeting someone for the first time.

2 Sorry?   b When you've made a mistake.

3 I'm terribly sorry.   c When someone is going away.

4 Happy New Year!   d When someone has had a baby.

5 No thanks, I'm just looking.   e On someone's birthday.

6 Have a good trip.   f When someone says thank you to you.

7 How do you do?   g When someone offers you some cake.

8 I'd love some but I'm on a diet.   h When a shop assistant offers to serve you.

9 Don't mention it.   i On 1st January.

10 Congratulations.   j When you didn't hear what someone said.

7 Adverbs of frequency Rewrite the following sentences using words from the table below.

every	two weeks	twice	a week
	4 months	3 times	a month
			a year

Example   We send out publicity brochures in January, April, July and October.
We send out publicity brochures every 3 months.

1   I take clients out Wednesdays and Fridays.

_____

2   I travel to Corby on the 1st and the 14th of every month.

_____

3   We have appraisal meetings in January, May, and September.

_____

4   I go jogging on Mondays, Wednesdays, and Saturdays.

_____

8 Reading Every country has its own customs. Read these descriptions of some different social and business customs. Can you identify which nationality group they refer to? Match each description with one of these nationalities.

the Japanese   the French   the Italians   the Germans   the Spanish   the British

1   They are happy to borrow manners and style from anywhere as long as it is useful and, above all, elegant. They love new things; their homes and offices are full of gadgets. Interactive video telephones, high speed trains, and modern architecture cause excitement not shock.

2   They leave work as punctually as they arrive and rarely take work home. They work hard, but statistically they put in fewer hours than fellow Europeans.

3   Lunches and dinners are an important part of business life. They are used to create personal relationships, and to make sure that the chemistry is right and that people can trust each other. Until coffee is served, they do not discuss business.

4   It is impolite to be exactly on time. For social occasions, this means arriving between ten and twenty minutes after the arranged time. Sometimes invitations specify, '7.30 for 8.00', which means you should not arrive later than 7.50.

5   They regularly work on Saturdays, don't often take more than a week's vacation, and count sick days as holiday.

6   The backbone of the economy is the thousands of small and medium sized private firms in the North. Their owners prefer independence, and it is more profitable to keep things in the family, pay workers in cash, and employ people who are officially self-employed, in order to make bigger profits and avoid strikes.

Source: *Mind Your Manners: Managing Business Cultures in Europe* by John Mole, Nicholas Brealey Publishing, London 1995.

Is there a description here for your country? If there is, do you agree with it? Why/Why not? If there isn't, can you write your own description?

7 Meetings

1 Holding a meeting

Choose the right words in *italics* to complete the conversation.

Jane   We need to *argue / discuss* [1] the problem of quality with the new LT60 components. *Basic / Basically* [2], we have two alternatives. We can either accept a wastage rate of 10% *or / and* [3] we can delay the schedule and redesign the component. *Any / Some* [4] views on this, Mark?

Mark   Yes, the important thing here is the timing. The customers can't wait any longer for this product. It's 90% OK. I *think / propose* [5] we should go ahead with production.

Jane   How do you *think / feel* [6] about that, Tom?

Tom   *I / I'm* [7] disagree. Waste costs money. We need zero defects.

Mark   But we haven't got time. *Aren't / Don't* [8] you agree, Jane?

Jane   I'm sorry, but I think Tom *has / is* [9] right. I don't think we should start production until the design is OK.

2 Recommending action

Read the problems, then select an alternative to recommend and give your reasons. You can invent your own reasons.

Example   Problem: Staff aren't using computers to their full potential.
Alternative 1: Send staff on training courses.
Alternative 2: Hire an in-company instructor.
Action: *I don't think we should hire an instructor because it's very expensive. I think we should send staff on training courses because it's more cost-effective.*

1   Problem: Late payments from a major client.
Alternative 1: Refuse to supply more goods until they pay their invoices.
Alternative 2: Offer a longer credit period to the client.

Action: _____

_____

2   Problem: Advertising expenditure rose by 26% last year.
Alternative 1: Reduce the amount of advertising we do.
Alternative 2: Hire a different advertising agency.

Action: _____

_____

3   Problem: To cut costs, we must make 100 staff redundant.
Alternative 1: Make the 100 most recent employees redundant (i.e. last in first out).
Alternative 2: Make the 100 least efficient employees redundant.

Action: _____

_____

4   Problem: Our competitors are headhunting our best managers.
Alternative 1: Offer all our top managers a large pay increase.
Alternative 2: Employ an agency to headhunt our competitors' best managers.

Action: _____

_____

3 Decisions Read the situations below and say what's going to happen.

Example Interform's headquarters are in central London. Office rents rose by 26% last month. The directors are looking at some new offices outside London today.
The directors are going to relocate their headquarters.

1 Leighton Dairies want to buy some new bottling machinery, but they don't have enough money. The Managing Director has an appointment with the bank manager tomorrow.

_____

2 Mrs Wright is in a restaurant with a client. They finished their meal a few minutes ago. She's signalling to the waiter.

_____

3 Corvent plc want to expand their freight transport service. The share price of Transpo plc, another freight company, is low at the moment. Corvent is buying up a large number of Transpo shares.

_____

4 Mr Lawson has a temperature of 40°C. It's 2.30 p.m., and he's picking up his briefcase and putting on his coat.

_____

5 Rivolet Ltd have a problem. Their main competitor cut their prices by 30% last week. Rivolet's Sales Manager has called an emergency meeting for this afternoon.

_____

4 Wordcheck Complete the puzzle and find the key word in 12 down.

Across
1 I need a haircut. Is there a _____ near by? (12)
2 There are 3 grass and 3 hard tennis _____ in the grounds. (6)
3 There's a _____ restaurant here that does good fish dishes. (7)
4 The hotel's got a _____ with weight training equipment. (9)
5 You can have a snack at the bar or a meal in the _____ (10)
6 Please return your keys to _____ when you leave. (9)
7 I want these trousers cleaned. Is there a _____ service? (7)
8 My name's Ward, and I have a _____ for 3 nights. (11)
9 If you want to buy presents, there's a _____ shop in the foyer. (4)
10 For a sandwich and a coffee, try the _____ bar. (5)
11 In the evenings you can dance in the hotel _____. (11)

Down
11 All good hotels offer this. (4, 7)

5 Speaking at meetings

Fill in the blanks with the correct phrases and sentences from the list below.

Can we get back to the main point?	... I didn't follow what you said.
Shall we get started?	What do you mean by ... ?
Shall we move on?	Let's turn to ...
Are we all agreed?	We need to discuss ...

1   Right, everyone's here. _____?

2   **A** Our training budget is less than 5% of the extra 2.5% VAT that comes on top of the original 15% on the 18,300 brochures at £2.47.

    B I'm sorry, _____.

3   It seems then that a price rise of 5.4% is the best solution. _____? Good.

4   **A** By the way, I saw Pete in the pub the other day. He moved house last weekend. Did you know? He told me ...

    B _____?

5   OK. We all agree on that item. _____?

6   Right, then, we can offer a commission of 12%. _____ the next item on the agenda.

7   There are three items on the agenda. Firstly, _____ the problem of late payments.

8   **A** There are some unusual things happening in the Finance Department.

    B _____ unusual?

6 Making suggestions

Suggest three different solutions to these problems.

Example   We've got some meetings with clients from Tokyo, but none of us speaks Japanese.
A *We could learn Japanese.*
B *Shall we get an interpreter?*
C *Why don't we see if they can speak English?*

1   We need to get these papers to head office before tomorrow morning.

    A _____

    B _____

    C _____

2   We need to improve office security. There were three thefts last month.

    A _____

    B _____

    C _____

3   We need to increase our market share.

    A _____

    B _____

    C _____

7 Reading   Complete the passage using the correct words from the box.

agenda
proposal
alternatives
views
agree
should
waste
opinion
people

One Man's Meet is Another Man's Poison

There are many different sorts of business meeting, and how the participants behave varies from country to country. In France meetings are generally used for briefing and co-ordination rather than discussing _____[1] and making decisions. They follow a detailed _____[2], and comments are well thought out rather than spontaneous. The same is true at formal meetings in Germany, where you _____[3] be well prepared if you wish to express an opinion. In the UK, on the other hand, participants often arrive at meetings unprepared, and papers distributed beforehand will not be read. This does not prevent anyone from expressing an _____[4] or putting forward a _____[5], though. Everyone is expected to contribute their _____[6].

SO WE'RE ALL AGREED OUR IMAGE IS A PROBLEM. SHOULD WE EMPLOY A PUBLIC RELATIONS CONSULTANT?

COVEN AGM

Meetings in Italy seem to be the most informal in Europe. They don't usually follow an agenda and _____[7] often come and go as they please. In fact, sometimes Italian meetings are more like a social gathering, used to reinforce a sense of togetherness.

It's very different in Spain, where meetings do little to create a team spirit. The Spanish prefer to be independent and make decisions on their own. Meetings are often a _____[8] of time because it is impossible to get everyone to _____[9].

8 Memorizing Words

? ? Q ? ? ? ? U ? ? ? ? I ? ? ? ? Z ? ?

Memorizing new words is one of the biggest problems people face
when they try to learn a language. Are you employing
the best memorization techniques?
Try this quiz and
find out.

	A		B
1 Which is better?	to study for one hour a day for eight days	or	to study for eight hours in one day?
2 Which is better?	to study for six hours with no break	or	to study for five hours - taking a five-minute break every half hour?
3 If you are trying to learn a long list of words, should you:	start at the top and work your way down, then go back up again and keep repeating the process	or	start at the top, work a short way down, then return to the top and start again and work your way down the list in this way?
4 Which memorization technique is more effective?	saying words aloud over and over again until you know them	or	using the sounds of the words to dream up mental pictures?

5 Which list is easier to learn?

beer	car	horse		cat	knife	paper
green	money	leg		dog	fork	pencil
business	book	history	or	tea	salt	black
clock				coffee	pepper	white

Now turn to page 76 to check your answers.

8 Making Arrangements

I Timetables

Central Travel Services

5 Alfred Street
London WC1
Tel: 0171 222 5800
Fax: 0171 222 6869

Confirmation of flight details

Mrs C. Bromhill
Customer No. 3176350002

Flight No.			Date	Time
			21 JUNE	2100H
BA 526	DEP. LONDON HEATHROW		22 JUNE	1730H
	ARR. SINGAPORE		28 JUNE	1530H
BA 530	DEP. SINGAPORE		28 JUNE	2100H
	ARR. LONDON HEATHROW			

Passengers are advised to check in at least 90 minutes before the stated departure time.

Claire
The flight takes 13 hours, so make sure you've got a good book!
J

Asian Agricultural Trade Fair

Singapore
June 23 to 27

Open daily:
8am-6pm

Information for Visitors

Airport transfers

A courtesy coach will collect visitors from the airport every 45 minutes and take them to the Mandarin and Sheraton Hotels.

A manager is discussing her visit to a trade fair with her secretary. Use the information in the letter to write her questions and the secretary's replies.

Example   When/the flight/from London/leave?

Q *When does the flight from London leave?*
A *It leaves at 9 p.m.*

1   What time/the plane/arrive/in Singapore?

Q _____

A _____

2   How often/coaches/go to/the hotel?

Q _____

A _____

3   When/the fair/start and finish?

Q _____

A _____

4   What time/it/open and close every day?

Q _____

A _____

5   When/the flight back/leave?

Q _____

A _____

6   When/it/get in?

Q _____

A _____

2 Arrangements

Ms Turner and Mr Wilson are trying to arrange a meeting. Look at their appointments for the week, and complete their conversation using each of these verbs only once.

meet	do	give	interview	attend	see	show	~~visit~~	pick up

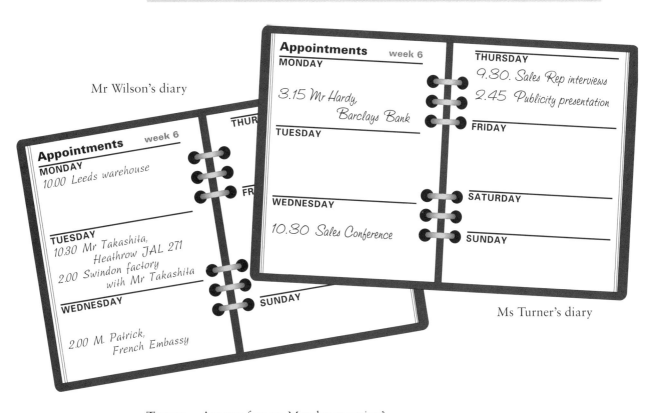

Mr Wilson's diary

Appointments week 6
MONDAY
10.00 Leeds warehouse

TUESDAY
10.30 Mr Takashita,
Heathrow JAL 271
2.00 Swindon factory
with Mr Takashita

WEDNESDAY
2.00 M. Patrick,
French Embassy

Appointments week 6
MONDAY
3.15 Mr Hardy,
Barclays Bank

TUESDAY

WEDNESDAY
10.30 Sales Conference

THURSDAY
9.30. Sales Rep interviews
2.45 Publicity presentation

FRIDAY

SATURDAY

SUNDAY

Ms Turner's diary

Turner	Are you free on Monday morning?
Wilson	No, _I'm visiting_ our warehouse in Leeds. What about the afternoon?
Turner	I'm afraid I can't make that. I _____[1] Mr Hardy at the bank. How about Tuesday?
Wilson	I'm busy all day Tuesday. In the morning I _____[2] Mr Takashita from Heathrow, and in the afternoon I _____[3] him round the Swindon factory. Would Wednesday morning suit you?
Turner	No, I'm tied up. I _____[4] the Sales Conference, but I'm free in the afternoon.
Wilson	I can't manage Wednesday afternoon. I _____[5] someone at the French Embassy. Are you busy on Thursday?
Turner	Yes. In the morning I _____[6] sales reps and in the afternoon I _____[7] a talk. _____[8] anything on Friday morning?
Wilson	No, I'm free then. Shall we meet at, say, 9.30?
Turner	That would be fine.

3 Wordcheck

Complete the puzzle and find the key word in 13 down.

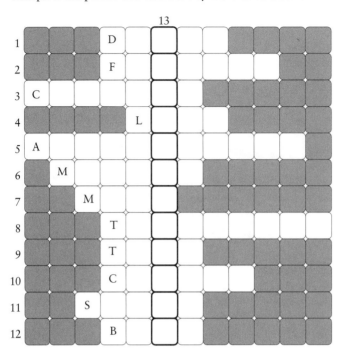

Across

1 I don't know if I'm free on Friday. I'll check my _____. (5)
2 I look _____ to meeting you next Friday. (7)
3 I'm ringing to _____ our meeting next week – is it still all right with you? (7)
4 He was half an hour _____ because of the traffic. (4)
5 Mr Turner rang and made an _____ to see you next week. (11)
6 Are you free on Thursday? No, I'm afraid I can't _____ Thursday. (6)
7 I'm afraid I can't _____ it this afternoon – I've got to go to London urgently. (4)
8 She picked up a _____ from the station to check the train times. (9)
9 I can't see you on Thursday afternoon – I'm _____ up. (4)
10 Could you _____ my appointment with the Marketing Manager? I'm afraid I won't be able to make it. (6)
11 Friday at 3.30? Let me see. Yes, that _____ me. (5)
12 I can't manage Tuesday – I'm afraid I'm _____.(4)

Down

13 Plans you make with other people. (12)

4 Time puzzle

A French saleswoman was in the UK on business. She phoned a taxi company and booked a cab for a certain time. She pronounced the time correctly and the English taxi company heard correctly, but the taxi arrived thirty minutes early. What time did she book the taxi for? What time did it arrive?

Clue: In Europe it's common to use the 24-hour clock but it's less usual in the UK.

5 Your arrangements

Look at your diary and write down sentences about your future plans and arrangements.

Example   *On Wednesday at 8pm I'm attending a Rotary Club meeting.*

6 Conversations

Put these two telephone conversations into the correct order.

A ☐ Oh. Would you like to change it then?

☐ Hello, Mr Parker. This is Matthew Brown.

☐ Fine. I'm sorry to mess you around like this.

☐ Well, let's say the 26th then, shall we?

[1] John Parker.

☐ I'm calling about our appointment on the 25th. I'm afraid something's come up.

☐ No problem.

☐ Thank you. Goodbye.

☐ Good morning, Mr Brown. What can I do for you?

☐ Could I? I'm free on the 24th or the 26th.

☐ I look forward to seeing you on the 26th, then.

B ☐ That's right.

☐ That'd be lovely. Thanks.

☐ Rosemary! How nice to hear from you. How's Tony?

☐ Great. Until Saturday then. Bye.

☐ You know where we live, don't you?

[1] John Parker.

☐ He's much better, thanks. In fact, we're having a party next Saturday. Would you like to come?

☐ John, this is Rosemary.

☐ Around nine, if that suits you.

☐ Russell Drive, isn't it?

☐ What time shall we come?

7 E-mail

A More and more people are communicating by e-mail and joining conferences on line. They often use abbreviations to save time. Do you know what these ones mean? Fill in the missing words.

1	IMO	In my o_____.	(I think)
2	OIC	Oh, I s_____.	(Now I understand)
3	NOYB	None of your b_____.	(It doesn't concern you)
4	TTYL	T_____ to you later.	(I'll speak to you later)
5	BBL	Be b_____ later.	(I'll return later)
6	HSIK	How should I k_____?	(I have no idea)
7	OTL	O_____ to lunch.	(Gone to lunch)
8	LOL	L_____ out loud	(Ha ha ha!)

B Emoticons are used in e-mail to show emotions and pass on visual information about the user. You have to read them with your head on one side.

Example   : -) The user is happy

Look at some more emoticons. Which one means the user:

1	is sad?	a	8 -)
2	is surprised?	b	: - o
3	has a moustache?	c	: - (
4	wears glasses?	d	[: -)
5	is listening to a personal stereo?	e	. -)
6	has one eye closed?	f	: - =)

9 Describing Trends

I Describing graphs

Read the reports on the sales results of different divisions of Sony and match each one to the correct graph.

1 **Music Group** sales went up slightly in 1991, then fell slightly in 1992 and 1993. But best-selling record releases by Michael Jackson, Billy Joel, Mariah Carey, Pearl Jam and many other artists led to a recovery in 1994.

2 There was a sharp increase in **Audio Equipment** sales in 1991 and another increase in 1992. But European market conditions were difficult in 1993 and 1994 and as a result, sales fell.

3 **Other** sales increased steadily between 1990 and 1994 as a result of the strong performance of semiconductors, telephones and CD-ROM drives.

4 There was a dramatic rise in **Pictures Group** sales in 1991 and sales continued to increase in 1992 and 1993. But the strong yen resulted in a fall in 1994. In fact, hit films such as *Sleepless in Seattle* and *Philadelphia* resulted in a rise in sales on a local currency basis in the US where we achieved a 19% market share.

5 **Video Equipment** sales rose sharply in 1991 but then fell in 1992 and 1993. The decline in the camcorder market led to a further sharp drop in 1994.

6 **Television** sales went up in 1991 and continued to rise steadily until 1994 when they dropped slightly. This was in spite of the fact that sales of computer displays and wide-screen TVs were strong.

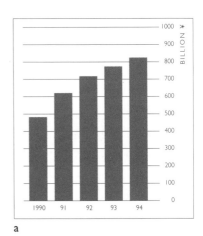

a

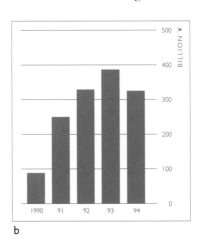

b

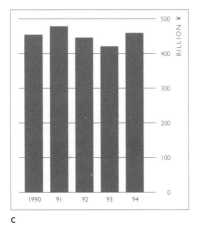

c

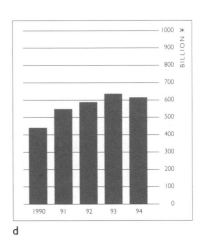

d

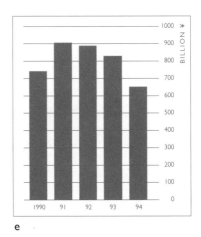

e

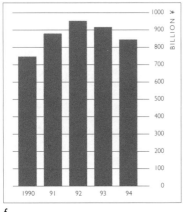

f

2 Money

We can *spend* money and we can *save* it. But we can do a lot of other things with money too. Find 14 more verbs we can use with the word *money* in the square. You can read some from left to right, some from top to bottom and some diagonally.

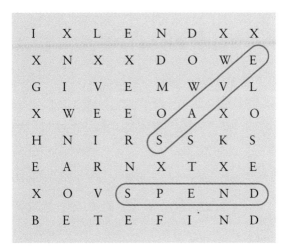

3 Wordcheck I

Complete the sentences with a word from the list below.

borrowed	made	gave	invest	owed	saved	spent	wasting

1 In 1990 the group _____ £4m from investments in overseas companies.

2 The accountants advised us to repay 15% of what we _____ to the banks.

3 The shareholders criticized the board for _____ so much money on unnecessary trips abroad.

4 The company _____ £5,000 to a local school to set up a computer department.

5 My stockbroker suggested I should _____ in a South East Asia Unit Trust.

6 The government _____ over £3.5m on a research and development project.

7 The government _____ £6.5 billion from the IMF for a construction project.

8 We _____ £323,500 in administrative costs by reducing the number of office staff.

4 Sales results

A Choose the correct words in italics to complete this report.

8

SALES

SALES ANALYSIS

Sales began the year at 30,000 units in January and increased
slight / slightly [1] to 32,000 units in February. There was a
sharp / sharply [2] rise *to / by* [3] 38,000 in March *due / led* [4] to the
introduction of a new price discounting scheme. This was followed by
a *slight / slightly* [5] fall in April when sales dropped to 36,000 units.

Our competitors launched a rival product in the spring and this
resulted *in / from* [6] a *dramatic / dramatically* [7] fall to 25,000 in May. But
we ran a summer advertising campaign and sales increased
steady / steadily [8] *to / by* [9] 2,000 units a month throughout June, July
and August until they stood *in / at* [10] 33,000 in September.

The *dramatic / dramatically* [11] rise to 45,000 in October resulted
in / from [12] the launch of our new autumn range. But then we
experienced problems meeting demand and sales fell *sharp / sharply* [13]
in November and remained *steady / steadily* [14] *at / by* [15] 39,000 in
December.

22

B Use the information in the report to complete this graph.

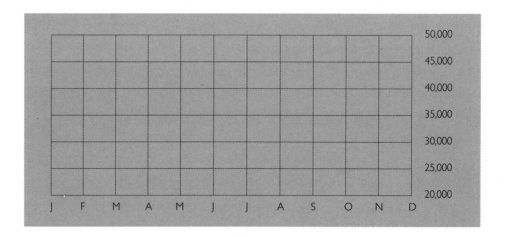

5 Wordcheck 2

Complete the puzzle and find the key word in 9 down.

						9			
1	I								
2					C				
3				D					
4				U					
5			E						
6		C							
7			W						
8			P						

Across

1 The rate of _____ shows how fast prices are rising. (9)
2 _____ spending increases when the public has more money. (8)
3 He paid all his _____ and now he has no money left. (5)
4 The _____ figures show how many people are out of work. (12)
5 Goods which are sold abroad are classified as _____ . (7)
6 There's a fixed _____ of £30 a week for electricity. (6)
7 We pay the staff their _____ on Fridays. (5)
8 Does the price include _____ and packing? (7)

Down

9 Banks charge their customers _____ on the money they borrow. (8)

6 Reading activity

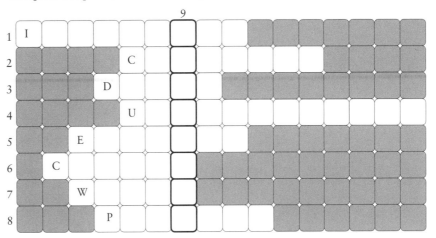

IS YOUR NUMBER UP ?

136
150
?
158

Look at the diagram, work out the logic and discover what number should replace the question mark ?

The answer is __ __ __

If you can solve this puzzle you could be eligible to join Mensa the high IQ society.

Cut the coupon for further details and a copy of the self - administered test.

Post to : Mensa, FREEPOST, Wolverhampton. WV2 1BR

Name _____
Address _____
_____ **Mensa**
Post Code _____

7 Reading

Number Power

SOME PEOPLE SAY IT MAKES NO SENSE, but numbers play an important part in many lives. That's why the Driver and Vehicle Licensing Centre has decided not to allow the number 666 on car number-plates because it is the mark of the devil.

OTHER NUMBERS HAVE GREAT SUPERSTITIOUS POWER – just ask triskaidekaphobics – people who fear the number 13 and Friday 13th in particular. Thanks to them, elevators all over the country jump from floor 12 to floor 14. On Concorde, you won't find Row 13, and many hotels have no floor 13.

AT THE SAVOY HOTEL, they are very careful. If there are 13 guests to dinner, the waiters bring an extra 'guest' – a small black cat made of stone called Kaspar – to make the numbers up to 14. According to the story, a South African businessman, Woolf Joel, went ahead with a dinner for 13 people in 1898 after the 14th guest cancelled. Joel was murdered soon afterwards.

PEOPLE WHO STUDY NUMBERS say that each number relates to one of the planets and that your birthday has a special meaning. To find out what numbers are important to you, write down your birth date. The day describes your outer personality, the month is your inner self and the year is your future. Where there is more than one figure, add them together to get a single figure. For example, $1965 = 1 + 9 + 6 + 5$ which is 21. Then add $2+1$ to get 3.

WORK OUT YOUR IMPORTANT NUMBERS and complete the chart below.

1 Sun – a great creator, outgoing, strong.
2 Moon – imaginative, sensitive.
3 Jupiter – ambitious, optimistic, positive.
4 Uranus – intelligent, scientific, often misunderstood.
5 Mercury – good communicator, quick thinker.
6 Venus – sensual, passionate, romantic.
7 Neptune – impatient, good learner.
8 Saturn – caring, understanding, but susceptible to problems.
9 Mars – strong, brave, passionate.

1 Birthday _____   Total _____   Outer self _____

2 Month _____   Total _____   Inner self _____

3 Year _____   Total _____   Future _____

1 Irregular verbs

Complete the chart.

Infinitive	Past tense	Past Participle
go	went	gone
buy		
		done
	fell	
grow		
lose		
		made
	rose	
		sold

2 Wordcheck

Complete the crossword.

Across

2 With these new pension plans, you can afford to take _____ retirement – you can stop work at 55. (5)

4 The people who work for a company. (5)

7 The company is expanding and they are looking for _____ employees. (3)

8 During the harvest, farmers take _____ hundreds of casual workers. (2)

9 The staffing levels at the Harrow branch have gone _____ because we are expanding our operation there. (2)

11 The _____ age in the UK is 60 for women and 65 for men. (10)

13 The Manager at the factory had to _____ three men for serious misconduct. (7)

15 The Directors have decided to _____ workers from the Slough to the Northampton factory. (8)

16 They plan to reduce the workforce by natural _____ . (7)

Down

1 As a result of the closure, all the workers at the car plant were made _____ . (9)

3 The Personnel department has _____ five new trainees who will begin work next month. (9)

5 Mr Henderson no longer works for us – he has _____ early retirement. (5)

6 The Chief Accountant resigned from the company _____ personal reasons. (3)

10 The Chairman of the Board _____ because he disagreed so strongly with the new proposals. (8)

12 I am pleased to report that we have achieved the _____ reductions in staffing levels. (6)

14 The Accounts Executive was _____ after he lost one of our most important clients. (5)

3 The latest news

Match the newspaper headlines with the articles.

1 **Cheers in 3D**

2 **'Hello, yes, thankyou, goodbye'**

3 **Old recruits**

4 Waste economics

5 **Hands up and dial a number**

6 *Stealing from the competition*

A ___

A builder and a menswear retailer have set up a spare-time business, making and marketing shoulder holsters. But these holsters are not for gunslinging detectives. They are designed for executives with mobile phones. Maurice O'Sullivan, who runs the business, has sold 2,500 since Christmas, many of them to overseas buyers. 'A lot of women buy them for their husbands,' he says, ' because they're fed up with torn pockets'.

B ___

HOW WELL do you have to speak a foreign language to do business abroad? Henning J. Caesar of ICI Clor-Chemicals has suggested seven words and phrases are all you need. They are: hello, goodbye, please, thank you, yes, no, and my friend will pay. 'As a marketing man with many years' experience in overseas travel,' he says, 'I feel we should concentrate on essentials'. Thank you and goodbye.

C ___

■ ■ ■ The Royal Society have included a new category in this year's Better Environment Awards. The new award will go to companies with bright ideas on recovering waste. 'The main problem with waste recovery projects is economics rather than technology,' says Scheme Director Helen Holdaway. 'The successful applicants must show their projects are economically viable.'
■

D ____

Meister 60, the Osaka engineering company, has found an unusual way to solve the Japanese labour shortage problem. It has been recruiting older people. 'The oldest applicant is 70,' says President Shigeo Hirano. 'A couple of applicants were 58, but we turned them down because they were too young.'

E ____

HMV Music have opened new warehouse-sized stores in Manhattan, on the doorstep of competitor Tower Records. But Russ Solomon, President of Tower Records, isn't worried about the competition. He has told his shareholders, 'If HMV have any good ideas, we'll steal them.'

F ____

Restaurant chain **TGI** have found a new marketing gimmick for their first UK advertising campaign. They are using three-dimensional printing. A set of 3-D viewing glasses will be bound into magazines so that readers can look at a waiter who appears to be offering them a tray of cocktails.

4 How about you?   Write an article about your company's latest news.

5 Targets

Item	Year to date	Last year
Catalogues	2	1
Special promotions	15	19
Mailshots	25	14
Presentations	38	41
Advertising expenditure	£386,000	£342,000
Rise in turnover (%)	+11%	+8%

The Director of a software publishing company is discussing this year's performance with the Advertising Manager. Write their questions and answers about the figures.

Example   catalogues/we/write?
Q *How many catalogues have we written this year?*
A *We've written two.*
Q *How many catalogues did we write last year?*
A *We wrote one.*

1 special promotions/we/run?

_____

_____

2 mailshots/we/do?

_____

_____

3 presentations/we/give?

_____

_____

4 How much money/we/spend on advertising?

_____

_____

5 How much/our turnover/rise?

_____

_____

6 Reading

It's not easy to understand a company's annual report. You often have to read 'between the lines' to find out what's really happening. Read this report (and the light-hearted explanations) and find out how well this company is really doing.

A STATEMENT FROM THE CHAIRMAN

■ ■ ■

This year, we have streamlined our operations
This year we have sacked a substantial number of staff

and engaged in aggressive marketing activities.
and raised our prices.

Home sales have shown a strong performance,
Home sales have at least reached their target,

but export sales have shown only moderate growth.
but export sales are well below forecast.

At present,
Right now,

we are restructuring our overseas marketing activities.
we are spending less abroad but hoping to sell more anyway.

Altogether, it has been a year of mixed fortunes
We've had a few disasters this year,

and consolidation.
and no growth.

We have seen the benefits of rationalization,
Staff reductions have saved money,

but we expect a challenging year ahead.
but we're not sure we can survive the next year.

11 Planning

1 Strategic planning

A A company is planning to build a new warehouse in Holmes Chapel. Read the briefing notes and list the advantages and disadvantages of the site.

HOLMES CHAPEL
WAREHOUSE AND
DISTRIBUTION CENTRE
Briefing Notes

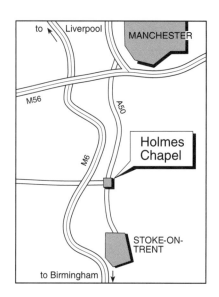

Strategic Location

Holmes Chapel is situated on the A50, one mile from the M6 motorway. Located in the centre of England, it is only 45 minutes from Manchester, 60 minutes from Liverpool, 70 minutes from Birmingham, and 3 hours from London. The town has a higher than average level of rainfall but snow is unusual and we do not expect bad winters to affect communications.

The town

The town of Holmes Chapel has a population of 6,000. There are 2 factories producing wallpaper and chemicals and a few small light industrial units. It is not in an enterprise zone and there are no government subsidies available. The unemployment rate is low. There are a large number of farms around the town and agriculture is the main source of employment in the area.

The site

The 2.5 hectare site provides plenty of space for the development. At present it is completely undeveloped with no mains services. We plan to lay pipes for gas, electricity, and water before we begin Phase 1 of the development in July.

B Complete these sentences about Holmes Chapel using words from the box.

rain	unemployment	people living in Holmes Chapel
snow	heavy industry	government subsidies
farms	agricultural workers	space for development
factories	gas or electricity	buildings on the site

There's a lot of (1) _____

There are a lot of (2) _____

There isn't much (3) _____

There aren't many (4) _____

There isn't any (5) _____

There aren't any (6) _____

2 Dialogues

Complete the dialogues with *some*, *a*, *much*, or *many*.

Example
A Good morning. I'd like _some_ French francs. How _many_ are there to the pound?
B Seven point seven at today's exchange rate. How _much_ money would you like to change?

1 A Who are your main competitors?
   B We haven't got _____. We offer _____ very unusual service. There aren't _____ companies operating in our field.

2 A How was the trip?
   B It was _____ disaster. Unfortunately, I didn't have _____ time, so I didn't meet _____ people.

3 A I'm not making _____ progress with this project. I really need _____ help.
   B I'm sure we can get you _____ extra staff. How _____ people do you need?

4 A I've got _____ message for you. Head Office want _____ report on the Antwerp project.
   B Oh no! I've already got too _____ work to do.

5 A I'm having _____ trouble arranging the conference – there isn't _____ accommodation in Thierre.
   B Get in touch with the Chamber of Commerce. They'll probably know _____ hotels we can use.

6 A There's _____ job in the paper you should apply for – look.
   B It sounds interesting, but I haven't got _____ experience of that kind of work.

3 Your future

Where will you be in ten years from now? Make sentences.

Example
same department
I think I'll be in the same department.
or
I don't think I'll be in the same department.

1 with the same company _____
2 in the same job _____
3 in a more responsible position _____
4 in the same house _____
5 in the same country _____
6 able to retire _____
7 (still) married _____

4 Wordcheck

Complete the puzzle and find the key word in 11 down.

Across

1 We'll need a hotel that has 24-hour room _____ . (7)
2 We'll need a _____ that can hold eighty people. (4)
3 We'll want a hotel with a good _____ for dinner. (10)
4 We'll want them to provide _____ at 9.00 and 11.00 and tea at 4.00. (6)
5 We'll need a slide _____ for the presentations. (9)
6 And the speakers will need a _____ so we can all hear them. (10)
7 Make sure that the bedrooms have all got _____ bathrooms as well. (2, 5)
8 We'll need to organize some _____ for the evening – perhaps a theatre trip. (13)
9 We'll want a good _____ too – don't go over budget. (5)
10 We'll need plenty of parking _____ for people who come by car. (5)

Down

11 We'll need all these things for this year's annual _____ . (10)

5 Giving advice

Read the situations below and give advice. Use *You'd better ...* or *You'd better not ...* and give a reason.

Example A colleague needs to attend a meeting starting in five minutes. She isn't ready yet.
You'd better hurry up or you'll be late.

1 One of your colleagues has a very important job interview this afternoon. She can't decide what to wear.

_____

2 A friend bought shares in Allied Steel. Today's headlines say 'Allied Steel make a £25m loss'.

_____

3 A colleague is feeling unwell. He has an appointment with an important client.

_____

4 Your friend notices the brakes on her car are not working very well.

_____

6 Plans

A publishing company is planning a new magazine for men. Read the notes and write sentences about their plans.

Title	*London Man*
Target audience	men aged 18–25
Circulation target	50,000 copies per week
Articles	sport, work, sex, health, fashion
Issues per year	52
Launch advertising	TV
Cover price	£2
First issue	mid-October.

Example   intend / call
They intend to call the magazine 'London Man'.

1   aim/sell/to

_____

2   hope/sell

_____

3   intend/have

_____

4   aim/publish

_____

5   plan/advertise

_____

6   plan/charge

_____

7   hope/publish

_____

7 Reading   What do you think the world will be like in the year 2020? In Japan several projects are already on the drawing board.

Arriving at a space hotel?

Japan 2020

THE GOVERNMENT in Japan has set up twenty-six research cities, or 'technopolises' to study new technologies. Scientists and entrepreneurs will live in these cities, and each city will carry out research of a different kind. For example, in Hiroshima they will study ecology, and in Kagoshima they will develop new bioceramics. The Japanese government will spend over $2.5 billion on each city over the next thirty years.

At Marinopolis, in Ohio Prefecture, they are already working on new ways of farming fish. They hope that one day they will be able to train fish to come to the fishermen. They will play underwater music to young fish when they are feeding, and then they will put them into the sea. When the fish are bigger, the fish farmers will sail out to sea and play the music, and the fish will come to the nets.

Private businesses will pay for research and development costs as well. Japan is interested in space and space travel, and Seishi Suzuki, director of the Shimizu Corporation, will build a space hotel. He hopes that his first guests will arrive there in 2015, and he already has a promotional video showing what the hotel will look like. His guests will stay in air-conditioned rooms and will take photos of the Earth from their windows.

12 Comparing Information

1 Making comparisons Complete the table.

Adjective	Comparative	Superlative
cheap	cheaper	the cheapest
expensive	more expensive	the most expensive
big		
	more powerful	
		the most modern
	better	
		the worst
far		

2 Comparing three companies Study these statistics about three North American publishing companies. Write answers to the questions below.

Newspapers	Sales $US millions	Profits $US millions	Earnings per share 1984-94 annual rate	No. of employees
The *New York Times*	2,358	213	5%	12,800
The *Tribune*	2,155	242	10%	10,500
The *Washington Post*	1,614	170	9%	6,800

Example   Which companies have the largest and smallest turnovers?
The New York Times has the largest and The Washington Post has the smallest.

1   Which companies have made the most and the least profit?

2   Which companies have the highest and the lowest earnings per share?

3   Which companies have the most and the fewest employees?

3 Comparing two companies

Complete the passage with the correct comparative form of the adjectives in brackets.

COMPARISON

PEACH COMPUTERS and CALCULO MACHINES, two giants of the computer industry, have decided to merge. Peach is a much _____[1](young) company than Calculo but it has had _____[2](fast) growth in recent years. It is now slightly _____[3](big) than Calculo. Peach's sales organization is _____[4](competitive) than Calculo's. It is _____[5](large) and plays a _____[6] (important) role in the organization. The Peach management team feel that they are _____[7](hard-working) and _____[8](innovative) than the Calculo team.

Calculo, on the other hand, is a _____[9](traditional) company. The managers are generally _____[10](old) than the managers in Peach and they have worked for the company _____[11](long). The Calculo managers feel they are _____[12](experienced) and that the company has a _____[13](good) reputation for product quality. They feel they may be _____[14](slow) than Peach, but they are right more often.

4 Comparing with as ... as

A Now make sentences comparing the two companies above. Use *as ... as* and these words:

old	traditional	aggressive	competitive	innovative	large

Example   *Peach Computers isn't as old as Calculo Machines.*

1 _____

2 _____

3 _____

4 _____

B Read the mottos of each company, then answer the questions.

A   The one who stays in front is the winner.
B   It is better to be second and right, than first and wrong.

Which motto belongs to which company?

Which motto do you agree with the most? Why?

5 Comparing consumption 1

Look at the graph and complete the sentences with the correct national group.

| The Hungarians | The French | The Japanese | The Germans | The Belgians |

Beer Consumption   Litres per head

Country	Litres per head
Germany	143
Czechoslovakia	132
Denmark	126
Belgium	119
Austria	118
Luxembourg	116
New Zealand	115
Britain	111
Australia	111
Hungary	101
USA	90
Japan	47
France	39

Source: Brewer's Society, 1988

1 _____ drink the most beer.

2 _____ drink the fewest litres per head.

3 _____ drink less than the Australians but more than the Americans.

4 _____ drink less per head than the Danes but more than the Austrians.

5 _____ drink the least beer, with the exception of the French.

6 Comparing consumption 2

Look at this graph and complete the sentences with the words below.

| less | the least | more | the most | fewer |

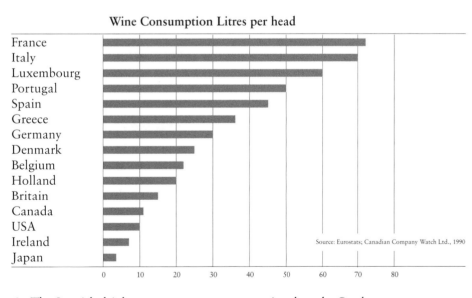

Wine Consumption Litres per head

Source: Eurostats; Canadian Company Watch Ltd., 1990

1 The Spanish drink _____ wine than the Greeks.

2 The Germans drink _____ wine than the Italians.

3 The Japanese drink _____ wine.

4 The French drink _____ wine.

5 The Belgians drink _____ bottles per person than the Danes.

7 Reading   **A** Do you agree or disagree with these statements?

	My opinion	Writer's opinion
1 People are naturally creative if you give them a chance.	agree / disagree	agrees / disagrees
2 Managers should tell workers what to do and how to do it.	agree / disagree	agrees / disagrees
3 People working at all levels of an organization should meet regularly to exchange information and plan improvements.	agree / disagree	agrees / disagrees
4 Companies need a centralized management to make decisions.	agree / disagree	agrees / disagrees
5 Employees prefer it when the management make all the decisions and they don't have a lot of responsibility.	agree / disagree	agrees / disagrees

B Now read the article and decide if the writer agrees or disagrees with them.

Participatory management, management by objectives, management by teams, quality circles – whatever you want to call it – is changing the traditional styles of management.

In brief, the philosophy is that you set free the natural creativity of people at all levels of the organization by encouraging them to set corporate goals, giving them what they need, and then leaving them alone to do the job.

The fuel that makes all this work is team spirit. Teams are formed vertically and horizontally so that all parts of the organization participate in sharing information and planning improvements.

Traditional authoritarian management disappears.

In its place is decentralization and authority and responsibility are placed at the lowest possible level.

For the organization, the results will be new ideas for products and services, better and more cost effective methods of working and greater productivity at less cost.

For the employees, the benefits are greater self-fulfilment, a chance to progress, and a happier and smoother-running work place.

More organizations are finding that employees at all levels can be a source of innovative and profitable ideas.

C Look for words in the article to complete the table below.

Noun	Adjective
authority	authoritarian
innovation	
profit	
tradition	
	creative
corporation	
	responsible
	productive
	beneficial

D Choose an adjective or noun from the table above to complete these sentences.

1 He's going to change the system completely with his fresh, new,

   i_____ ideas.

2 After-sales made a loss last year but they're going to make a small

   p_____ this year.

3 He prefers to do things in the old t_____ way.

4 We need to look for a c_____ solution to this problem.

5 The c_____ bosses met to discuss the takeover.

6 The salary is low for such a r_____ position.

7 Automation of the plant has resulted in greater p_____ .

8 Management by objectives is b_____ to the company as a whole

   and the individuals who work in it.

1 Air travel

Match words from list A to words from list B to make nine compound nouns.

Example   1 f *departure lounge*

A		B	
1	departure	a	desk
2	travel	b	Express
3	duty-free	c	flight
4	long-haul	d	class
5	economy	e	luggage
6	boarding	f	lounge
7	hand	g	shop
8	check-in	h	card
9	American	i	agency

2 Travel arrangements

Now complete this memo, using the compound nouns from Exercise 1. Use each compound noun once.

M E M O R A N D U M

From: P. Larsen

Date: 21 January

To: J. Harriet

Subject: My flight to Japan last week

Why did you buy me an _____¹ ticket for my trip to Japan? I know we have to save money, but it was a _____².

When I got to Gatwick airport, there was a long queue at the _____³. I had to wait half an hour to get my _____⁴, and they only allowed me to take one small piece of _____⁵ onto the plane. I was late going into the _____⁶, so there was no time to visit the _____⁷ and buy the clients a present.

On the plane, the seats were small and uncomfortable, and I couldn't sleep or do any work. When I arrived in Tokyo, I was tired, jet-lagged, and unfit for the meeting. I needed to change my ticket for the flight home, but the _____⁸ told me I couldn't. I had to buy a new one which was very expensive. I paid by _____⁹ and travelled first class.

Please refund the attached invoice.

3 Travel information

Complete the passage using these verbs:

| can | must | mustn't | don't have to |

Travel information Heathrow Airport

Car parking You _____ ¹ leave your car unattended on roads outside the terminals or the police will remove it. Long-stay car parks for Terminals 1, 2, and 3 are located off the North Perimeter Road.

You _____ ² book in advance as there is always space available.

Taxis You _____ ³ hire a taxi outside the terminal buildings 24 hours a day. If the journey is 20 miles or less, taxi drivers _____ ⁴ accept the hire and _____ ⁵ charge more than the fare shown on the meter. For journeys of more than 20 miles, drivers _____ ⁶ accept the hire if they don't want to. But, they _____ ⁷ charge a special rate so you _____ ⁸ negotiate the fare before starting the journey.

4 Obligations

Write sentences using the words in brackets. Use *mustn't* or *don't have to*.

Examples   This information is highly confidential. (tell anyone) *You mustn't tell anyone*.
This report isn't urgent. (finish it today) *We don't have to finish it today*.

1   These clients are very important. (upset them in any way)

_____

2   We have arranged car hire at the airport for you. (forget your licence)

_____

3   You can pay by credit card if you like. (pay cash)

_____

4   We've guaranteed zero defects. (make any mistakes)

_____

5   They can deliver very fast. (order it straight away)

_____

6   You can spend the weekend in Athens if you like. (be back until Monday)

_____

7   We can't afford more than $6,000. (offer $7,000)

_____

8   They speak good English. (employ a translator)

_____

5 Your job

Write sentences about what you have to do and don't have to do at work.

Example   clock in
I don't have to clock in.

1 work late most evenings _____

2 work at weekends _____

3 share an office _____

4 type my own letters _____

6 give presentations in English _____

6 Wordcheck

Complete this puzzle about travel and transport and find the key word in 10 down.

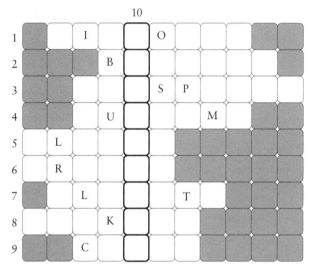

Across

1 What are Charles de Gaulle, JFK, and Gatwick? (8)
2 What can be excess, hand, or lost? (7)
3 What can be valid for ten years, out of date, or British? (9)
4 Where can you be stopped, go through the green channel, or have something to declare? (7)
5 What can land, take off, or crash? (6)
6 What can be derailed, high speed, or late? (6)
7 What can you miss, catch, or change? (7)
8 What can be single, return, or APEX? (7)
9 What can be boarding, business, or credit? (5)

Down

10 What can be first class, tired, or unaccompanied? (9)

7 Conditionals

Put the verbs in brackets into the Present tense or the Future using *will*.

A What time does Mr Tanaka's flight arrive at Heathrow?

B He gets in at 10.30 tonight. If he _____[1](take) about half an hour to get through customs, we _____[2](leave) just after 11.00. Then we _____[3](get) to the hotel just before midnight if there _____[4](not/be) any problems.

A I'm afraid there probably will be problems. I phoned the airport, and the weather's bad. If it _____⁵(not / improve), there _____⁶(be) some long delays.

B That's OK. If he _____⁷(be) late, I _____⁸(wait) for him.

A Yes, but if the fog _____⁹(get) worse, they _____¹⁰(start) diverting flights to other airports. If he _____¹¹(land) in Manchester and there _____¹²(be) nobody there to meet him, he _____¹³(not / be) very pleased.

B I'm sure he _____¹⁴(understand) if that _____¹⁵(happen). I'll go to Heathrow, and if his flight _____¹⁶(not / arrive), I _____¹⁷(find out) what's happening.

8 Reading   Read the following true story. Do you know any similar stories?

The least successful traveller

The least successful traveller on record is an Italian, Mr Nicholas Scotti. In 1977, Mr Scotti set off from San Francisco to fly to Italy. On the way, his plane stopped at Kennedy Airport for an hour to refuel. Mr Scotti thought he was in Italy and got out. He then spent two days in New York, believing he was in Rome.

Scotti expected his friends to meet him at the airport, and when they didn't arrive, he tried to find his own way to their address. As he travelled round the city, he was surprised to see that many of Rome's historic monuments had disappeared, but decided it was due to modernization. He also noticed that many people spoke English with an American accent. It didn't worry him, because he assumed that Americans got everywhere. That also explained why there were so many English street signs.

Scotti had to ask a policeman the way to the bus depot, and of course, he asked in Italian. By chance, the policeman was a native of Naples, and he replied, of course, in fluent Italian.

He travelled around on a bus for twelve hours until the driver delivered him to a second policeman, and that was when the argument started. Mr Scotti was amazed that the Rome police force could employ someone who didn't speak a word of Italian. Even when everyone told him he was in New York, he refused to believe it. To get him back to San Francisco, the police drove him to the airport at top speed, with sirens screaming. 'You see,' said Scotti to his interpreter, 'I know I'm in Italy. That's how they drive here.' ★

14 Company Visits

I Corporate development

Write sentences about Anzec using the words below and the information in the graph.

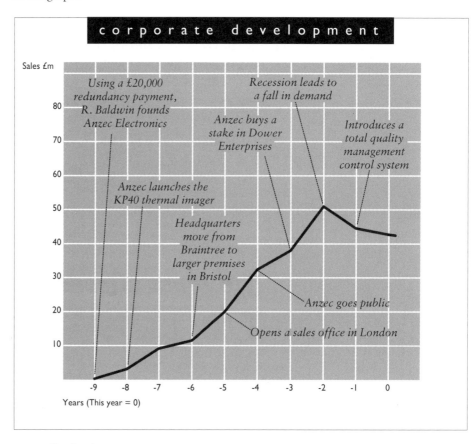

corporate development

Sales £m

Using a £20,000 redundancy payment, R. Baldwin founds Anzec Electronics

Recession leads to a fall in demand

Anzec buys a stake in Dower Enterprises

Introduces a total quality management control system

Anzec launches the KP40 thermal imager

Headquarters move from Braintree to larger premises in Bristol

Anzec goes public

Opens a sales office in London

Years (This year = 0)

Example Anzec / be / in business
Anzec has been in business for nine years.
It / produce / the KP40
It's been producing the KP40 for eight years.

1 Anzec / be / based in Bristol

   _____

2 It / have / sales office in London

   _____

3 Anzec / be / a public limited company

   _____

4 Anzec / own / a stake in Dower Enterprises

   _____

5 Anzec / suffer / from the recession

   _____

6 The company / operate / a TQM control system

   _____

2 A career history

> **Career Résumé: M. S. Karlssen**
>
> 1975 – 78   University of Stockholm (majored in Psychology)
> 1978 – 84   Consultant in a child psychiatric hospital
> 1984 – 95   Employed by Elmqvist Competence Search,
>   a recruitment agency
>
> **Recent career moves**
> August 1995   Became self-employed
>   Set up own recruitment consultancy
> October 1995 Opened an office in Malmo
> February 1996 Won a major contract with a computer company

Answer these questions about Mr Karlssen's career.

Examples   How long did he study psychology?
            He studied psychology for three years.
            How long has he been running his own company?
            He's been running his own company since August 1995.

1   How long ago did he leave university?

_____

2   How long was he a consultant at the psychiatric hospital?

_____

3   How long has he been self-employed?

_____

4   How long has he had an office in Malmo?

_____

5   How long did he work for the firm of recruitment consultants?

_____

3 How about you?   Answer these questions about yourself.

1   How long ago did you start your present job?

_____

2   How long have you had your present job?

_____

3   How long ago did you start learning English?

_____

4   How long have you been learning English?

_____

4 Error correction

Study these sentences. Three are correct and three have grammatical mistakes. Find the mistakes and correct them.

1 The company I work for is in business for twenty years.
2 They've been a plc for the early eighties.
3 I've been working in the London office since February.
4 Before that, I worked in the Manchester branch for six years.
5 They've been expanding the London operations since the last six months.
6 Since Christmas, several employees have had to transfer from Manchester to London.

5 Experience

A A chemical company is recruiting a sales manager to work in South America. Read the interviewer's notes.

CANDIDATE: *Celia Hill*

POST: *Sales Manager, Chile*

EXPERIENCE OF WORKING FOR A LARGE MANUFACTURING COMPANY:

Yes, with British Aerospace (1984-90) and Total (1990-present)

EXPERIENCE OF A POSITION OF RESPONSIBILITY:

Yes, Assistant Sales Manager (1988-90) and Sales Manager (1990-present)

EXPERIENCE OF A CHEMICAL INDUSTRY:

Yes, she had a job with ICI before she went to college.

EXPERIENCE OF LIVING AND WORKING ABROAD:

No, and she can't speak Spanish either.

B Complete the passage. Put the verbs into the Past Simple or the Present Perfect.

In some ways Ms Hill is an ideal candidate for this post. She is knowledgeable, intelligent, and adaptable. She has ___has had___(have) sales experience with two large manufacturing companies: She ___worked___(work) for British Aerospace for six years, and she _____[1](work) for Total since 1990. She _____[2](be) an assistant sales manager for two years at BA and _____[3](be) a sales manager since she joined Total. She has also had direct experience of the chemical industry. She _____[4](have) a job with ICI before she went to college. The problem is she _____[5](never live) abroad. She _____[6](never learn) Spanish either. She speaks Italian well, but that's no use in Chile.

6 Irregular verbs Complete the table.

Infinitive	Past tense	Past participle
make	made	made
	grew	
		built
	took	
pay		
	put	
		left
shake		

7 Passives Match the phrases in column A with those in column B to make eight true sentences.

A

1 Many of the world's cars

2 Most of the world's rubber

3 Sony

4 Nearly all the world's pink diamonds

5 Nobel Peace Prizes

6 German interest rates

7 The New York Stock Exchange

8 The currency of Ethiopia

B

a are mined in Australia.

b are awarded every year.

c is situated in Wall Street.

d are set by the Bundesbank.

e is grown in Malaysia.

f is called the Birr.

g are built by robots.

h is based in Japan.

8 Processes

A Study the flow chart and the article describing a relocation counselling service, and fill in the missing information below.

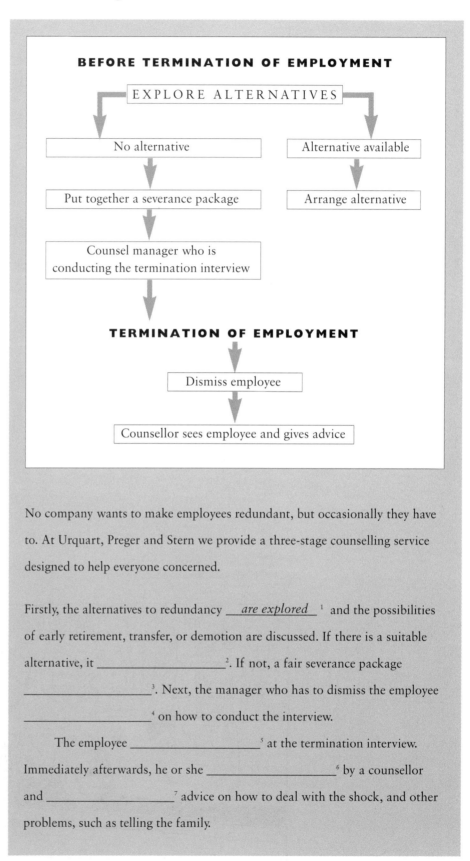

No company wants to make employees redundant, but occasionally they have to. At Urquart, Preger and Stern we provide a three-stage counselling service designed to help everyone concerned.

Firstly, the alternatives to redundancy ___*are explored*___ [1] and the possibilities of early retirement, transfer, or demotion are discussed. If there is a suitable alternative, it _____[2]. If not, a fair severance package _____[3]. Next, the manager who has to dismiss the employee _____[4] on how to conduct the interview.

The employee _____[5] at the termination interview. Immediately afterwards, he or she _____[6] by a counsellor and _____[7] advice on how to deal with the shock, and other problems, such as telling the family.

B Now read the rest of the article and complete the flow chart.

The following day, there is a second interview to assess the employee's strengths and weaknesses and administer aptitude tests. The counsellor then analyses the test results and discusses them fully with the employee. They also advise on financial matters, if necessary. Over the next few weeks, the counsellor helps the employee to work out a job search plan, and provides advice on applications, CVs, and interview techniques. Working together, they identify suitable companies for applications and the counsellor offers support and assistance to the employee during the first interviews. If the company wishes, continued support can be given until the employee is successful in finding a new job.

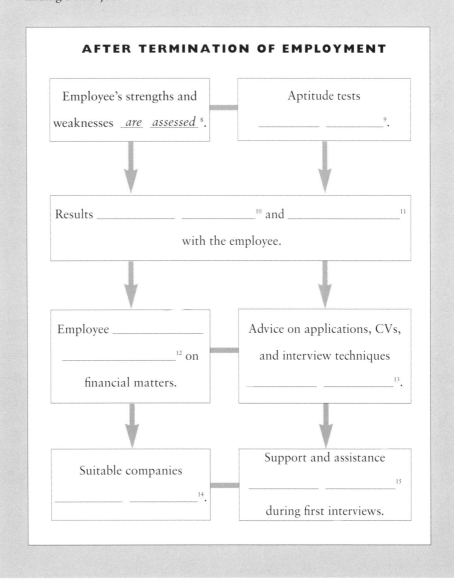

AFTER TERMINATION OF EMPLOYMENT

| Employee's strengths and weaknesses _are_ _assessed_ [8]. | Aptitude tests _____ _____ [9]. |

Results _____ _____ [10] and _____ [11] with the employee.

| Employee _____ _____ [12] on financial matters. | Advice on applications, CVs, and interview techniques _____ _____ [13]. |

| Suitable companies _____ _____ [14]. | Support and assistance _____ _____ [15] during first interviews. |

15 Tackling Problems

1 Conditionals

Match the two halves of these sentences.

1   If someone read my personal mail,

2   Companies wouldn't spend so much on advertising,

3   If I won a great deal of money,

4   I would apply for a job like that,

5   Their staff would feel much happier,

6   If I knew how to solve the problem,

a   if their offices weren't so small and dark.

b   I wouldn't need to employ a consultant.

c   if it didn't work.

d   I would probably still work part-time.

e   I'd be very angry.

f   if I had the right qualifications.

2 Reaching an agreement

Complete these conversations. Use the phrases below.

Supposing we agreed to …	That's rather high.
Could you be more specific?	… did you have in mind?
… check what we've agreed?	… we couldn't accept that.
… that might be possible.	

1 **Supplier**   The price is $978.

    Customer   Really! _____

2 **Customer**   We expected the price to be lower.

    Supplier   Did you? What price _____

3 **Customer**   If we paid for delivery, would you reduce the price?

    Supplier   Yes, _____

4 **Supplier**   I'm afraid we can only offer a 5% discount.

    Customer   _____ 5%. Would you pay for installation?

5 **Customer**   We'd like you to improve the payment terms.

    Supplier   _____

    Customer   Yes. We'd like a longer credit period.

6 **Supplier**   If we sent the goods by air instead of by sea, would you pay the
extra cost?

    Customer   No, I'm afraid _____

7 **Supplier**   Is that everything, then?

    Customer   I think so. Could we _____

3 Wordcheck   Complete the puzzle and find the key word in 10 down.

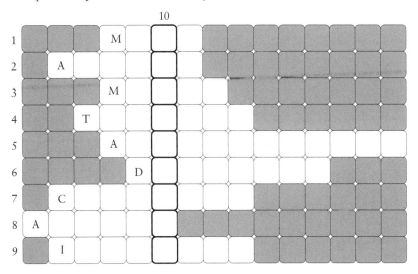

Across

1 Those are our standard terms, as I've said. What price did you have in _____? (4)
2 If we _____ to a unit price of $55, what credit terms could you offer us? (6)
3 We can't offer a 3-year warranty, but a 2-year warranty_____ be possible. (5)
4 Before we finish, could we just go _____ what we've agreed once again? (7)
5 If a client doesn't agree to a proposal, the negotiator will suggest some _____. (12)
6 What _____ will you give me on the list price? (8)
7 The price is reasonable and it _____ favourably with our competitors. (8)
8 A two-week credit period is too short. I'm afraid we couldn't _____ that. (6)
9 If we placed a larger order would you _____ the discount to 15%? (8)

Down

10 Try to reach an agreement by discussion. (9)

4 Consequences   **A** Write sentences explaining the consequences of these actions.

Example   we employ an assistant → we don't fall behind schedule.
If we employed an assistant, we wouldn't fall behind schedule.

1 we employ untrained staff → it enables us to reduce our wage bill
2 we don't check the invoices → we pay them more quickly
3 we keep larger stocks → we don't run out of any lines.
4 we don't update our computer system → it saves a lot of money
5 we employ more people → we don't have to work so hard.

B All the actions could have bad consequences as well as good. Invent more endings to the sentences. Explain the possible bad consequences. Complete these sentences using your own ideas.

Example   If we employed an assistant, *we'd have to pay another salary.*

1 If we employed untrained staff …
2 If we didn't check the invoices …
3 If we kept larger stocks …
4 If we didn't update our computer system …
5 If we employed more people …

5 Reading game

Are you a good manager ?

Read number 1 and choose the best solution from A, B, or C. Then follow the instructions. If you read *Go to 10*, then read the next part of the problem under 10. If you read *Go to 8*, then read number 8. Continue until you find the best solution to the problem. Use a dictionary if you need any help, and good luck!

You are the manager of a mail order company with about 30 employees, over half of them women. One morning a group comes to you to ask the company to set up a crèche* to look after the children. Would you:
A explain that you don't have to do this by law and that it is too expensive. *Go to 10*
B agree to set up a crèche – it would keep the employees happy. *Go to 8*
C say you will look into the matter. *Go to 6*

Why are you reading this?
Read the instructions once more and try again.

The group reports back with the figures. They show that a small crèche for 4 children can be run for about £10,000 per year. Would you:
A go ahead and set up the crèche. *Go to 4*
B ask the finance department to check the figures. *Go to 8*

Staff morale is very high. After 2 years, the demand for the crèche is even bigger. There are now 11 children. It costs £40,000 a year, and the cost is rising. Would you:
A limit the crèche facilities to 10 places on a first come, first served basis. *Go to 7*
B allow the crèche to continue until you can find another solution. *Go to 11*
C close the crèche down. *Go to 17*

The head of Finance comes to you. He is an important person in the company. He says he cannot allow his staff to waste time with research like this – the women should do the study themselves. Would you:
A accept his decision. *Go to 3*
B say that the Finance Department must help the committee with the full study. *Go to 12*

You find that you do not have time to do the research yourself. Would you:
A ask the Finance Department to conduct a study. *Go to 8*
B ask the women themselves to come up with a proposal. *Go to 3*
C organize a committee made up from Personnel, Finance, and the women themselves. *Go to 5*

One of the directors is refused a place in the crèche. She is furious. Would you:
A make an exception in her case and give her a place in the crèche. *Go to 18*
B tell her that the company policy is clear, and that she cannot be helped. *Go to 9*

The Finance Department tells you that a crèche is out of the question – it is far too expensive. Would you:
A tell the women that, unfortunately, the company cannot offer child-care facilities. *Go to 17*
B form another committee to look at other proposals. *Go to 6*
C go ahead anyway; a crèche may be expensive, but you cannot afford to lose your workers. *Go to 4*

* a day nursery for very young children.

At a board meeting, the woman director calls for your resignation. You have made a mess of the company's finances and too many bad decisions. *Start again*

A number of women resign. The Personnel Department says you must do something about child-care; hiring new staff all the time is expensive. Would you:

A have another look at the problem. *Go to 6*

B ask the Finance Department to look at the problem. *Go to 8*

C ask the group of women to study the cost of a crèche. *Go to 3*

The Finance Department was right: the high cost of the crèche is affecting the company's finances very badly. Would you:

A close the crèche down. *Go to 17*

B cut the workers' salaries by 20%. *Go to 14*

C allow the crèche to continue until you can find another solution. *Go to 19*

The committee says that a crèche is the best solution, but the most expensive. An alternative is to pay for part of the cost of sending children to a local child-minder. (A child minder is someone who works at home and takes in children for the day.) Would you:

A go ahead with the crèche. *Go to 8*

B choose the subsidized child-minder. *Go to 15*

C ignore the problem and hope it will go away. *Go to 1*

The women realize why you have made your decision when they are told all the facts. They are pleased with the new system and it works well. Congratulations: you have found the best solution.

The head of the company calls you into his office. 'How did you get into this mess?' he shouts. *Start again*

Some staff don't like the child-minding scheme. Two of the women say they will resign if you do not choose a proper crèche. Would you:

A explain your decision fully at a company meeting. *Go to 13*

B accept the resignations. *Go to 16*

C change your mind and go ahead with the crèche. *Go to 11*

Your actions make the staff very unhappy. They think you are very unreasonable. However, there are no more resignations, and the scheme works well. This is one solution, but not the best. *Try again*

The women are angry with your decision. Seven of them hand in their notice. *Go to 14*

Three other members of staff ask for places in the crèche. You gave the director a place, so they want one too. Would you:

A create more places in the crèche. You must be fair to everyone. *Go to 19*

B say you cannot help. There is no money available. *Go to 17*

The company has had a bad year, and loses money. It is clear that the crèche costs too much money. Would you:

A keep to your decisions and carry on. *Go to 14*

B tell the women they must pay for part of the crèche themselves. *Go to 17*

6 If I had ...

Complete the sentences with your own ideas.

Example   If I had the chance to have a different career, *I would study medicine.*

1 I would have to move house if ...
2 If the traffic in the mornings wasn't so bad, ...
3 I would hand in my notice, if ...
4 If I asked my boss for a pay rise, ...
5 I would emigrate, if ...

7 Review

How fast can you read documents and find the information you need? Look back at the Student's Book to find the answers to these questions. There is one on each unit.

1   George Wong is the Chairman of
    a Sun Valley   b Parkview   c a Hong Kong Bank   d the Swire Group

2   Paul Carter's phone number is:
    a 29508   b 00 55 11 223 3181   c 91430 6687   d 03 408 441932

3   The number of new restaurants McDonald's open each day is
    a 1   b 3   c 5   d 7

4   A Cabstar pick-up weighs
    a 2,570 kg   b 11,815 kg   c 1,160 kg   d 3,370 kg

5   Which of the following numbers is considered unlucky in Japan?
    a 2   b 4   c 8   d 12

6   The country with the highest proportion of executives who drink port is
    a Sweden   b France   c Spain   d Great Britain

7   Simo Hattarri is
    a French   b Japanese   c Swedish   d Finnish

8   The restaurant on the ground floor of the Riverside Hotel is the
    a Swithins   b Marlborough   c Mange Tout   d Florence

9   Coca-Cola was invented in
    a Atlanta   b Chicago   c New York   d New Orleans

10 The joint venture between Graphic Images and Karstel concerns
    a optical disks   b finance   c distribution   d telecommunications

11 Club Med's conference venue in Phuket has
    a 6 restaurants   b 3 swimming pools   c no night club   d a sound system

12 The country with the highest rate of inflation is
    a China   b Russia   c Brazil   d Turkey

13 In Muslim countries, the working week starts on
    a Monday   b Tuesday   c Friday   d Saturday

14 A graphologist analyses
    a the stars   b numbers   c radioactivity   d handwriting

15 Mr Lee's flight arrives at
    a 3 o'clock   b 3.30   c 8 o'clock   d 3 am

ANSWER KEY

1 MEETING PEOPLE

1 First meetings

8   2   5   1   7   3   9   6   4

2 Jobs

1 an estate agent	5 a doctor
2 in computers	6 for Lego
3 a solicitor	7 an accountant
4 for Canon	8 in construction

3 Job titles

Answers depend on individual.

4 Companies

1 Mitsui - shipbuilding - Japan - yen
2 Jacobs Suchard - food - Switzerland - Swiss franc
3 Eastman Kodak - photographic equipment - USA - US dollar
4 Daewoo - electronics - South Korea - won
5 Michelin - rubber products - France - French franc
6 Rauma-Repola - forestry products - Finland - markka
7 Carlsberg - beverages - Denmark - kröne

5 Asking questions

A
1 How	3 who	5 Why
2 Where	4 When	6 What

B
1 Where does he come from / Where is he from?
2 Is he German?
3 Who does he work for?
4 What does he do?
5 What's his position / job?

6 Boardroom puzzle

The Managing Director is Peter, who is German, is sitting at the head. The Accountant is Bernadette, who is Swiss and sitting on his left. Opposite her is the English Lawyer, Nathan.

7 Commuting

A
1 London	4 two and a half hours
2 6.30	5 three friends
3 train	6 they all play *Trivial Pursuit*

B
1 does she work
2 does she leave home in the morning
3 does she travel to work
4 does it take
5 does she travel with
6 doesn't she get bored

8 Replies

1 b	3 j	5 d	7 c	9 e
2 h	4 a	6 g	8 i	10 f

9 Reading

1 d   2 a   3 f   4 b   5 c   6 e

2 TELEPHONING

1 Pronunciation

A
1 b / e	3 e / b	5 f
2 c	4 a	6 d

B
1 d	3 e	5 f
2 c	4 a	6 b

C
1 GDP	3 PLC	5 FOB
2 NEC	4 CIF	

2 Making calls

1 f   2 d   3 e   4 b   5 c   6 a   7 c

3 On the line

1 Extension	7 afraid	13 read
2 engaged	8 back	14 Anything
3 put	9 take	15 all
4 Who's	10 of course	16 welcome
5 Hold on	11 Could	
6 get	12 code	

4 Requests

A Asking other people to do things:
Could you ...
Can you ...
Would you ...

Asking if it's OK to do things:
May I ...
Can I ...
Could I ...

B
1 Could you tell me the time?
2 May I smoke in your office?
3 Would you give me a lift to the station?
4 Could I borrow your copy of the production plan?
5 Could I copy a file from your computer?
6 Could you lend me that book?

5 Wordcheck

1 call	6 extension	11 this
2 hold	7 speaking	12 sorry
3 moment	8 back	13 engaged
4 number	9 message	14 communication
5 Could	10 put	

6 Writing letters

A
1 With reference to
2 I am writing to confirm
3 I would be grateful
4 Could you possibly
5 Thank you for your help
6 I look forward to hearing from
7 Yours

B
1 Thank you for your letter of
2 I am writing to
3 I would be delighted to
4 I am afraid that
5 I am enclosing
6 Please contact us again if
7 I look forward to meeting you
8 sincerely

7 Reading

1 A and B are bank robbers. They are discussing the timing of a bank robbery and the vehicles they will use.
2 A is a secretary, Mary, and B is her boss. The boss is trying to avoid speaking to an unwelcome caller, but finally agrees to take the call.
3 A is a recorded message on an answering machine; B is a caller.
4 A and B are lovers. They are talking on the phone when B's boss walks past. B then quickly pretends to be talking to a customer / client.
5 A (Jane) is calling B from a phone box. Before Jane can give her number (so that B can call her back), the call is cut off because her phonecard has run out.
6 B (Mr Brown) is talking to his lawyer, A, about fees. At first Mr Brown misunderstands, and thinks the fees are £13,000, but then he realizes that A has actually said £30,000, much more than Mr Brown had expected.

3 COMPANIES

I Current projects

1 d	2 e	3 a	4 b	5 f	6 c

2 Present Continuous

1 are you calling	5 am writing
2 am staying	6 is visiting
3 are you doing	7 are you both staying
4 am collecting	

3 Facilities

A

1 Is there	4 Are there	7 Is there
2 Is there	5 Is there	
3 Are there	6 are there	

B

1 g	2 e	3 f	4 a	5 c	6 b	7 d

4 Asking questions

1 Q How many hotels are there near the centre?
  A There are six.
2 Q Is there an airport near the centre?
  A Yes, there is.
3 Q How far is Nice airport from Monaco?
  A Twenty-two kilometres.
4 Q How long does it take to get there by helicopter?
  A It takes seven minutes
5 Q How long does it take to fly there from Madrid?
  A It takes one hour and forty-five minutes.
6 Q Are there good rail and road links?
  A Yes, there are.

5 Present Simple and Continuous

Answers depend on individual.

6 Saying numbers

1 nineteen ninety
2 ten forty five
3 the twenty-first of January
4 seventeen and a half per cent
5 thirty-four pounds fifty
6 nought point five six eight three litres

7 Reading

1 KELLOGG'S	3 BASF	5 MICHELIN
2 MICROSOFT	4 PEPSICO	

8 Wordcheck

1 headquarters	5 consumer	9 range
2 staff	6 subsidiary	10 rent
3 warehouse	7 manufacture	11 joint venture
4 factory	8 turnover	

4 EXCHANGING INFORMATION

I Opposites

1 good-bad	6 young-old
2 big-small	7 interesting-boring
3 quiet-noisy	8 entertaining-dull
4 fast-slow	9 expensive-cheap
5 new-old	10 expensive-good value

2 Describing things

The three extra adjectives after the noun are suggestions only.

2 a computer	up-to-date expensive electronic
3 the weather	wet windy cold
4 a price	low reasonable fair
5 a hotel	cheap well-run family
6 a secretary	hard-working dedicated enthusiastic
7 an office	tidy disorganised air-conditioned
8 a company	well-managed bankrupt friendly
9 a car	electric fuel-efficient smart
10 a letter	well-written confidential personal

3 More adjectives

1 interesting	4 confusing	7 fascinating
2 interested	5 surprised	8 amused
3 excited	6 worrying	

4 Measurements

1 300.5 m tall	4 3,460 km long
2 1,615 m deep	5 70-72 beats / minute
3 8.85 km high	6 2,889 pages thick

5 Wordcheck

A 1 paper   2 job   3 efficient   4 wide

B 1 paper   2 efficient   3 wide   4 a job

6 Car problems

1 was	6 was	11 were
2 were	7 were	12 was
3 weren't	8 weren't	13 was
4 was	9 wasn't	14 was
5 was	10 was	15 was

7 Product specifications

1 How deep is it?
2 How wide is it?
3 How high is it?
4 How much does it weigh? / How heavy is it?
5 How much does it cost?

5 REPORTING

1 A career history

/d/	/t/	/ɪd/
studied	worked	attended
married	published	elected
specialized	replaced	defeated
retained		visited
survived		

2 Describing a career

1 began	9 adopted	17 helped
2 became	10 believed	18 had
3 used	11 earned	19 made
4 were	12 demanded	20 reported
5 appeared	13 worked	21 thought
6 joined	14 sold	22 ran
7 was	15 rented	23 gave
8 grew	16 insisted	

3 Irregular verbs

2 send-sent	6 fly-flew
3 pay-paid	7 feel-felt
4 make-made	8 learn-learnt
5 read-read	

4 Dates and times

Answers depend on individual.

5 Questions

A

1 Where – g	4 Did – c	7 Which/What – f
2 Why – d	5 How – h	8 Which/What – e
3 Who – a	6 When – i	9 Was – b

B 1 When did you phone her?
2 Why did he leave?
3 Where did he go?
4 How much did it cost?
5 Did you see the report?
6 How long did you stay?
7 Who did you speak to?
8 What was the weather like?

6 Your career

Answers depend on individual.

6 SOCIALIZING

1 Welcoming a visitor

1 to meet you
2 your first visit
3 have a good flight
4 eat anything on the plane
5 the restaurant or the hotel first
6 sort of food do you like
7 try some Greek food

2 Socializing

1 e	3 h	5 g	7 c
2 a	4 b	6 d	8 f

3 Wordcheck

1 steak - the others are ways of cooking
2 frozen - the others are ways of cooking potatoes
3 potato - the others are types of fruit
4 pea - the others are fish
5 lamb - the others are types of meat from pigs
6 margarine - the others are dairy products
7 bread - the others are vegetables
8 cooked - the others are ways of cooking steak

4 Menus

A 2 U 4 C 6 U 8 U 10 U
3 C 5 U 7 C 9 U 11 C

5 Free time

A 1 play 2 go 3 go 4 play 5 do

B Answers depend on individual.

6 Social expressions

1 e 2 j 3 b 4 i 5 h 6 c 7 a 8 g 9 f 10 d

7 Adverbs of frequency

1 I take clients out twice a week.
2 I travel to Corby twice a month / every 2 weeks.
3 We have appraisal meetings 3 times a year / every 4 months.
4 I go jogging three times a week.

8 Reading

1 the French 3 the Spanish 5 the Japanese
2 the Germans 4 the British 6 the Italians

7 MEETINGS

1 Holding a meeting

1 discuss 4 Any 7 I
2 Basically 5 think 8 Don't
3 or 6 feel 9 is

2 Recommending action

Answers depend on individual.

3 Decisions

1 The MD is going to ask for a bank loan.
2 She is going to ask for the bill.
3 Corvent plc is going to take over Transpo plc.
4 He is going to go home.
5 They are going to discuss cutting their prices too.

4 Wordcheck

1 hairdressers 5 restaurant 9 gift
2 courts 6 reception 10 snack
3 seafood 7 laundry 11 discotheque
4 gymnasium 8 reservation 12 room service

5 Speaking at meetings

1 Shall we get started?
2 ... I didn't follow what you said.
3 Are we all agreed?
4 Can we get back to the main point?
5 Shall we move on?
6 Let's turn to
7 we need to discuss
8 What do you mean by ...?

6 Making suggestions

Answers depend on individual.

7 Reading

1 alternatives 4 opinion 7 people
2 agenda 5 proposal 8 waste
3 should 6 views 9 agree

8 Memorizing words

1 (A) The golden rule is 'a little and often'.
2 (B) We learn more effectively if we take breaks.
3 (B) Psychologists have found it's better to rotate words frequently.
4 (B) In tests, visualization was found to be more effective that rote learning.
5 (B) It's a little longer than (A) but you will see that the words are grouped in pairs. Remembering one of the pair will help you remember the other. It can also help to form associations between different English words.

8 MAKING ARRANGEMENTS

1 Timetables

1 What time does the plane arrive in Singapore?
It arrives at 5.30pm.
2 How often do coaches go to the hotel?
They go every forty-five minutes.
3 When does the fair start and finish?
It starts on 23rd June and finishes on 27th June.
4 What time does it open and close every day?
It opens at 8am and closes at 6pm.
5 When does the flight back leave?
It leaves on the 28th June at 3.30pm.
6 When does it get in?
It gets in at 9pm.

2 Arrangements

1 I'm meeting / seeing	5 I'm seeing / meeting
2 I'm picking up	6 I'm interviewing
3 I'm showing	7 I'm giving
4 I'm attending	8 Are you doing

3 Wordcheck

1 diary	6 manage	11 suits
2 forward	7 make	12 busy
3 confirm	8 timetable	13 arrangements
4 late	9 tied	
5 appointment	10 cancel	

4 Time puzzle

She booked the taxi for 22.10 (twenty-two ten) but the taxi arrived at twenty to ten (21.40). The times sound the same - twenty-two ten and twenty to ten .

5 Your arrangements

Answers depend on individual.

6 Conversations

A 5   2   8   7   1   4   9   11   3   6   10

B 8   5   3   11   6   1   4   2   10   7   9

7 E-mail

A		
1 opinion	4 Talk	7 Out
2 see	5 back	8 Laughing
3 business	6 know	

B 1 c   2 b   3 f   4 a   5 d   6 e

9 DESCRIBING TRENDS

1 Describing graphs

1 c   2 f   3 a   4 b   5 e   6 d

2 Money

1 lend	6 find	11 have
2 owe	7 waste	12 make
3 give	8 lose	13 need
4 earn	9 invest	14 borrow
5 bet	10 win	

3 Wordcheck 1

1 made	4 gave	7 borrowed
2 owed	5 invest	8 saved
3 wasting	6 spent	

4 Sales results

A					
1 slightly	6 in	11 dramatic
2 sharp	7 dramatic	12 from
3 to	8 steadily	13 sharply
4 due	9 by	14 steady
5 slight	10 at	15 at

B

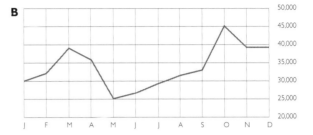

5 Wordcheck 2

1 inflation	4 unemployment	7 wages
2 consumer	5 exports	8 postage
3 debts	6 change	9 interest

6 Reading activity

Answer	151
Dog	45
Cat	38
Bird	30

10 PROGRESS UPDATES

1 Irregular verbs

Infinitive	Past tense	Past participle
go	went	gone
buy	bought	bought
do	did	done
fall	fell	fallen
grow	grew	grown
lose	lost	lost
make	made	made
rise	rose	risen
sell	sold	sold

2 Wordcheck

Across

2 early	8 on	13 dismiss
4 staff	9 up	15 transfer
7 new	11 retirement	16 wastage

Down

1 redundant	6 for	14 fired
3 recruited	10 resigned	
5 taken	12 target	

3 The latest news

1 F   2 B   3 D   4 C   5 A   6 E

5 Targets

1 How many special promotions have we run this year?
We've run fifteen.
How many special promotions did we run last year?
We ran nineteen.

2 How many mailshots have we done this year?
We've done twenty-five.
How many mailshots did we do last year?
We did fourteen.

3 How many presentations have we given this year?
We've given thirty-eight.
How many presentations did we give last year?
We gave forty-one.

4 How much money have we spent on advertising this year?
We've spent £386,000
How much money did we spend on advertising last year?
We spent £342,000.

5 How much has our turnover risen this year?
It has risen (by) eleven per cent.
How much did our turnover rise last year?
It rose (by) eight per cent.

11 PLANNING

1 Strategic planning

1 There's a lot of rain / space for development.
2 There are a lot of farms / agricultural workers.
3 There isn't much snow / unemployment.
4 There aren't many people / factories.
5 There isn't any heavy industry / gas or electricity on site.
6 There aren't any government subsidies / buildings on the site.

2 Dialogues

1 any / a / any
2 a / much / many
3 any / some / some / many
4 a / a / much
5 some / much / some
6 a / much

3 Your future

Answers depend on individual.

4 Wordcheck

1 service	5 projector	9 price
2 room	6 microphone	10 space
3 restaurant	7 en-suite	11 conference
4 coffee	8 entertainment	

5 Giving advice

There are lots of possibilities - here are some suggestions:

1 You'd better wear something smart.
2 You'd better get some financial advice.
3 You'd better cancel the appointment.
4 You'd better book it into a garage.

6 Plans

1 They aim to sell to men aged 18-25.
2 They hope to sell 50,000 copies a week.
3 They intend to have articles on sport, work, sex, health, and fashion.
4 They aim to publish 52 issues a year.
5 They plan to advertise on TV.
6 They plan to charge £2 a copy.
7 They hope to publish the first issue in mid-October.

12 COMPARING INFORMATION

1 Making comparisons

Adjective	Comparative	Superlative
big	bigger	the biggest
powerful	more powerful	the most powerful
modern	more modern	the most modern
good	better	the best
bad	worse	the worst
far	further / farther	the furthest / farthest

2 Comparing three companies

1 The *Tribune* has made the most profit and The *Washington Post* has made the least.
2 The *Tribune* has the highest earnings per share and The *New York Times* has the lowest.
3 The *New York Times* has the most employees and The *Washington Post* has the fewest.

3 Comparing two companies

1 younger		8 more innovative
2 faster		9 more traditional
3 bigger		10 older
4 more competitive		11 longer
5 larger		12 more experienced
6 more important		13 better
7 more hard-working		14 slower

4 Comparing with *as ... as*

A Possible answers:
1 Peach Computers isn't as traditional as Calculo Machines.
2 Peach Computers doesn't have as a good a reputation as Calculo Machines.
3 Calculo Machines isn't as competitive as Peach Computers.
4 Calculo Machines isn't as innovative as Peach Computers.

B A–Peach, B–Calculo

5 Comparing consumption 1
1 The Germans
2 The French
3 The Hungarians
4 The Belgians
5 The Japanese

6 Comparing consumption 2
1 more
2 less
3 the least
4 the most
5 fewer

7 Reading

A The writer's opinion:
1 agrees
2 disagrees
3 agrees
4 disagrees
5 disagrees

C Noun / Adjective
innovation / innovative
profit / profitable
tradition / traditional
creation / creative
corporation / corporate
responsibility / responsible
productivity / product
benefit / beneficial

D 1 innovative 4 creative 7 productivity
2 profit 5 corporate 8 beneficial
3 traditional 6 responsible

13 BUSINESS TRAVEL

1 Air travel
1 f 4 c 7 e
2 i 5 d 8 a
3 g 6 h 9 b

2 Travel arrangements
1 economy class
2 long-haul flight
3 check-in desk
4 boarding card
5 hand luggage
6 departure lounge
7 duty-free shop
8 travel agent
9 American Express

3 Travel information
1 mustn't 4 must 7 can
2 don't have to 5 mustn't 8 must
3 can 6 don't have to

4 Obligations
1 We mustn't upset them in any way.
2 You mustn't forget your licence
3 You don't have to pay cash.
4 We mustn't make any mistakes.
5 We don't have to order it straight away.
6 You don't have to be back until Monday.
7 We mustn't offer $7,000.
8 You don't have to employ a translator.

5 Your job
Answers depend on individual.

6 Wordcheck
1 airports 5 planes 9 cards
2 baggage 6 trains 10 passenger
3 passports 7 flights
4 customs 8 tickets

7 Conditionals
1 takes 7 is late 13 won't be
2 will leave 8 will wait 14 will understand
3 will get 9 gets 15 happens
4 aren't 10 will start 16 doesn't arrive
5 doesn't improve 11 lands 17 will find out
6 will be 12 is

14 COMPANY VISITS

1 Corporate development
1 Anzec has been based in Bristol for six years.
2 It has had a sales office in London for five years.
3 Anzec has been a plc for four years.
4 Anzec has owned a stake in Dower Enterprises for three years.
5 Anzec has been suffering from the recession for two years.
6 The company has been operating a TQM control system for a year.

2 A career history

1 He left university ___ years ago. *
2 He was a consultant at the psychiatric hospital for six years.
3 He has been self-employed since 1995 / for ___ years.*
4 He has had an office in Malmo since October 1995 / for ___ years.*
5 He worked for the firm of recruitment consultants for eleven years.

correct figure depends on the year now.

3 How about you

Answers depend on individual.

4 Error correction

1 The company I work for <u>has been</u> in business for twenty years.
2 They've been a plc <u>since</u> the early eighties.
3 Correct.
4 Correct.
5 They've been expanding the London operations <u>for</u> the last six months.
6 Correct.

5 Experience

1 has worked	3 has been	5 has never lived
2 was	4 had	6 has never learned

6 Irregular verbs

Infinitive	Past tense	Past participle
grow	grew	grown
build	built	built
take	took	taken
pay	paid	paid
put	put	put
leave	left	left
shake	shook	shaken

7 Passives

1 g   2 e   3 h   4 a   5 b   6 d   7 c   8 f

8 Processes

2 is arranged	7 is given	12 is advised
3 is put together	8 are assessed	13 is provided
4 is counselled	9 are administered	14 are identified
5 is dismissed	10 are analysed	15 are offered
6 is seen	11 discussed	

15 TACKLING PROBLEMS

1 Conditionals

1 e   2 c   3 d   4 f   5 a   6 b

2 Reaching an agreement

1 That's rather high.
2 did you have in mind?
3 that might be possible.
4 Supposing we agreed to
5 Could you be more specific?
6 we couldn't accept that.
7 check what we've agreed?

3 Word check

1 mind	5 alternatives	9 increase
2 agreed	6 discount	10 negotiate
3 might	7 compares	
4 through	8 accept	

4 Consequences

A 1 If we employed untrained staff, it would enable us to reduce our wage bill.
2 If we didn't check the invoices, we would pay them more quickly.
3 If we kept larger stocks, we wouldn't run out of any lines.
4 If we didn't update our computer system, it would save a lot of money.
5 If we employed more people, we wouldn't have to work so hard.

B Possible consequences are as follows:

1 If we employed untrained staff, they wouldn't know much about the job.
2 If we didn't check the invoices, we would make mistakes.
3 If we kept larger stocks, our costs would increase.
4 If we didn't update our computer system, the quality of our work would suffer.
5 If we employed more people, our wage bill would increase sharply.

5 Reading game

One possible solution is as follows:
1 C   6 C   5 B   12 B   15 A   13

6 If I had ...

Answers depend on individual.

7 Review

1 b	4 a	7 d	10 a	13 d
2 d	5 b	8 c	11 d	14 d
3 b	6 a	9 a	12 b	15a